C000180241

Why I Started a Small School

Why I Started a Small School

A nurturing, human scale approach to education and parenting

Rosalyn Spencer

Matador
9 Priory Business Park
Kibworth Beauchamp
Leicestershire LE8 0RX, UK
Tel: (+44) 116 279 2299
Fax: (+44) 116 279 2277
Email: books@troubador.co.uk
Web: www.troubador.co.uk/matador

ISBN 978 1783062 553

British Library Cataloguing in Publication Data.
A catalogue record for this book is available from the British Library.

Typeset in Minion Pro by Troubador Publishing Ltd
Printed and bound in the UK by TJ International, Padstow, Cornwall

Matador is an imprint of Troubador Publishing Ltd

For Alf,
without whose dedicated help and support the
nursery and small school would not have been possible.

'Everybody has intelligence …
it's just a matter of finding the right door …
and then finding the right key to unlock it!'

Professor Tim Brighouse

What people are saying about *Why I Started a Small School...*

"In Rosalyn Spencer's first book of her planned series of three, she takes the reader through the process of setting up a new school with the flair of a natural storyteller. *Why I Started a Small School* is an informative and entertaining read."
Martin Ouvry, Novelist and Editor.

"In this book Rosalyn Spencer narrates a powerful story of transformation in education. In the age when schools have lost their way this book shows that great ideals of education can be put in practice by parents, teachers and pupils joining hands and working together. I recommend this book to all educators wholeheartedly."
Satish Kumar, Editor-in-Chief of Resurgence & Ecologist, and Founder of The Small School, Hartland.

"'Looking back now', writes Rosalyn, 'the story is hard to believe'. And it is, but it's true, and written by someone who lived the idea that ordinary people can do extraordinary things – not just for themselves, but for others as well."
Kevin Holloway, Senior Lecturer in Education

"Rosalyn Spencer experienced a truly epic journey through our educational system, first as an apprehensive student, and later as a devoted parent and inspirational teacher. In her book, she weaves her experiences together to give us an inspiring case not just for change, but also for hope."
Ann Hickey, Social Worker and Parenting Specialist.

"This account of Rosalyn Spencer's struggle with the education system, on her own and on her children's behalf, leads her to take positive action. Today the government has at last come round to supporting groups of parents who want to start their own schools. That is in great part due to people like Rosalyn who were not prepared to accept a second-rate education. I am gratified to have played some small part in her inspirational story."

Colin Hodgetts, Former Headteacher of The Small School, Hartland

"Rosalyn Spencer's courageous establishment, in 1993, of an inclusive, nurturing, human scale small school, was a much-needed exemplar of change in education-provision, in what is now, a socio-ecologically fragmenting Britain. Were such qualities used, to inform the development of Government-funded, parent- and teacher-instigated Free Schools, this would greatly benefit future, UK social cohesion."

Stuart McBurney, Freelance Lecturer and Author of Ecology into Economics Won't Go *(Green Books)*

"Having taught in comprehensive schools for twenty-seven years I am aware of the problems that can arise, particularly in the transition from primary to secondary school. Rosalyn Spencer's account of her experience of school both as a student, then teacher and parent, highlights in a clear and balanced way the potential challenges and failings of the state system. Her vision and determination to seek a viable alternative in providing for her child's needs when the system had clearly failed, is admirable."

Steve Gosse, Former teacher

"Whatever position one takes in debates about parental choice, school structures and home schooling, or on controversial initiatives such as the introduction of Free Schools and Academies, Rosalyn Spencer's intensely personal and compelling narrative about her battle to establish a new type of school two decades ago marks her out as an innovator ahead of her time.

She reminds us of the importance of building schools and learning communities that embrace and engage parents and students as active partners and engaged citizens, rather than as distanced clients and complaining customers; this is the essence of any education (and any education system) that aspires to be human in scale and spirit."

Tony Breslin, Chair of Human Scale Education (2010-2014)

"The focal point of the book is that we all blindly follow the system despite its faults and failings but few, if any, of us have the courage to challenge it, moreover the guts to do something about it. Despite barriers, setbacks and opposition Rosalyn Spencer showed tremendous determination to give her children the best possible start in life, something every parent should aspire to."

Geoff Needham, Senior Executive, Regional Development Agency

Author's Notes

Apart from my own son and daughter (who are both in agreement), the names of other children have been changed to protect individual identities. Wherever possible, people who are mentioned by their actual name in the book have been contacted, and have given their consent to being included.

This book tells the story leading up to the opening of a new small school, and is the first in a trilogy. The next book: *The Small School Years* is about what actually happened during the years the school was running, and how lives were changed forever. The third book *An Educational Journey* is based on a ten week caravan trip I made around England and Scotland, with my two children (then aged seven and twelve), visiting seventeen different human scale small schools.

Contents

Foreword

by James Wetz
(Director of Human Scale Education
2011-2014)

This contribution from Rosalyn Spencer is extremely timely.

In the current policy environment with so much intense debate about the design and organisation of our schooling system, this book reminds us of the importance of parents having a voice in the shaping of schools for our children. It is a reminder that whilst parents have been cast as 'stakeholders' and 'consumers' they have a real and urgent part to play as 'learning partners' having a voice in the way children are raised and educated, and in the way our schools should be designed and organised.

This book makes a compelling case, as the narrative about how we might design our schools differently, is based in real experience. Rosalyn Spencer shares with us her upbringing and formation which led to her becoming a teacher, and with stories of real children and families illustrated with feeling and sensitivity, she shares with us almost unconsciously (in this first book in her trilogy), her passion about why we need to be rethinking our offer of schooling to children. The book tells of her dedication and courage to challenge the status quo and to argue for a different approach. Through the book, the values that inform the policy and practice that might be at the heart of a small school shine through – the importance of relationships, the place of creativity alongside rigour, the advantages of scale. It makes the argument which Human Scale Education supports: that while scale is important, size alone is not the predominant factor, rather, it is what we can do differently when using a smaller learning environment that is important.

Rosalyn Spencer's account of her journey – from childhood to professional training; becoming a parent and bringing up a family; and her career as a teacher – which were the necessary foundation of her struggle to develop a small school, is deeply personal and engaging. It is also a story where, implicitly, she acknowledges the importance of how small schools can create an experience of community that young children need to have if they are to become citizens of the future. Above all, it argues for an experience of schooling where the parental voice is strong, and which knows that what it wants from a school is not an institution where children are forced to conform to a system, but a community which responds to, and affirms, the interests and possibilities within each and every child.

For me this book captures essential truths espoused by two of the leading pioneers of the small school movement in the USA: 'You cannot teach a child unless you know that child well' (Ted Sizer – *Horace's Hope*) and 'Let's keep it simple so we can concentrate on the complexity of children and the complexity of the ideas we want them to engage with' (Debbie Meier – *The Power of their Ideas*)

This book is a reminder that there is an alternative to factory schools, and the warehousing of children in the name of education, and that individual parents with energy, vision, courage, perseverance and commitment, can make a significant contribution as part of a movement which argues for a human scale education to be the right of every child and parent.

Bristol, February 2013

Introduction

This is a book for parents everywhere, especially those who are worrying about problems their child may be encountering in school. This book may be the proof you need to know that it is not your fault, that you have done the very best you can for your child under the circumstances, and that perhaps the school needs to examine its methods.

This book is for teachers and childcare professionals too. If you already use a caring, human scale approach towards children and their parents, then this book will affirm what you are doing. If you are a teacher or professional who uses 'throw-away' comments and/or find yourself blaming the parents when things aren't working in the classroom, this book should help you to see things from a different perspective. Hopefully, it will encourage you to think again.

The book may be of great interest to adults who struggled through school themselves and left school with few (or no) qualifications and low self-esteem. It will give you the opportunity to reflect on your own schooling and examine whether your lack of success was really down to your lack of ability – or was it down to lack of encouragement and/or imagination on the part of your teachers?

Finally, this book is for anybody who enjoys reading memoirs and narrative non-fiction, especially if you have an interest in parenting and education.

Enjoy.

CHAPTER 1

The Letter
(1992)

It has been confirmed in writing, I am a terrible parent... it felt as if my whole world was falling apart around me. Leaning on the pine table to support myself, I slumped down onto one of the wooden chairs. Through the gothic-shaped windows of our second-floor kitchen, I barely noticed the large goods barge heading down-river towards Goole docks ... I had tried so hard to be a good parent. I thought I'd tried harder than most, and yet here was the proof: I was a failure. It felt as if somebody had stuck a dagger in my chest. How had I not seen the damage I was doing to my son? How had I managed to become so neglectful? Within moments of finishing the letter I was sobbing uncontrollably.

Before he had started school, Dan had been a bubbly, bouncy child. If anything, he was a little bit too cheeky and would never stop talking. I had read to Dan since he was a baby. Even before he could talk I used to cuddle him on my knee and read a book, pointing to the pictures and describing them. Dan used to love this. As he got a little older, he would climb into our bed in the early hours of the morning clutching a book and asking for it to be read to him. He clearly loved books.

Dan's sister, Nicki, had been born the very week he started school. The timing wasn't brilliant. To a young child it may have appeared that this baby was a replacement for him now he had started school. But my husband, Alf, and I gave Dan so much love and reassurance that we didn't think this was an issue for him.

A few hours after Nicki was born, Dan arrived at the hospital to see his new little sister for the first time. He looked incredibly cute in his smart school uniform and he beamed with pride at the thought of being big brother to this newly born baby. After a brief visual study of his sister, Dan opened his satchel and took out his homework. Much to our amusement, he started holding up colour flashcards a few inches away from Nicki's eyes, and clearly stated the correct colour of each one. He obviously wanted to give his baby sister an early start to her education and was determined to be her first ever teacher.

The Spencer family of three had become four, and so life went on. As the days went by, however, Alf and I started becoming increasingly worried about Dan. His love of books gradually changed into a loathing, and he always seemed unhappy and downhearted when he came home from school. We wondered where our bubbly little boy had gone.

Over the next year or so, we expressed our concerns to the school on a number of occasions. Each time, we were told that they had no particular worries about him and we were just being over-anxious parents.

By the time Dan was seven years old, the school finally agreed that he was behind most of his peer group with reading, but his class teacher dismissed my concerns in a light-hearted way, saying, 'He'll survive, he's bright enough!'

When I suggested to the headteacher that Dan might be dyslexic, he replied, 'Oh no – I've worked with dyslexic children, and there is no way that your son could be considered dyslexic.' I felt I couldn't really say anything else at that moment in time.

By the age of eight, Dan had become very withdrawn. He hardly ever made eye contact with people who were trying to communicate with him, and his responses were always minimal. His shoulders were permanently rounded, and he walked with his head bowed. He seemed a very unhappy child. What had gone wrong for him?

I sought information from the Dyslexia Association and attended training events that convinced me even more that Dan was indeed dyslexic. If I was correct, this meant Dan had a specific learning difficulty affecting his reading, writing and spelling ability. Dyslexia is not linked to an individual's intelligence but is the way that the brain processes information. I firmly believed that Dan really did need specialised support in school if his self-esteem was not going to diminish any further. Armed with leaflets and checklists that seemed to me to represent an excellent indicator of Dan's needs, the school finally agreed to him having a full educational assessment.

There had been a time when I used to have an excellent relationship with the school, but this had been tainted by my growing reluctance to accept their dismissal of Dan's problems, and their reluctance to consider that he may have any learning difficulties at all.

After the assessment process eventually started, I can recall having a meeting with one educational psychologist who seemed to confirm that Dan could be dyslexic. Weeks later nothing had changed at school and Dan was still struggling. When I queried the outcome, I was told that the psychologist concerned had left the authority and that his report couldn't be traced. Without consulting me, the school arranged for another educational psychologist to see Dan. The first I learned of any further action was when the letter arrived in the post containing what I believed to be inaccurate, and very hurtful, assumptions about Dan's family life. Was this based on the opinions of some of the teachers at the school, who had come to regard me as a troublesome parent, I wondered?

The letter, which was based on a short observation of Dan in the classroom, and – I'm assuming – consultation with teaching staff, stated categorically that although Dan was behind his peer group with reading and had difficulty with writing and spelling, he was definitely not dyslexic. The four-page letter indicated that Dan's difficulties at school could be a consequence of 'bruised self-esteem' as a result of his home life. It stated that Dan appeared to be an anxious child, and that he felt second best compared to his younger sister.

I felt that most of Dan's anxieties were due to the problems he was having in his school environment. The main problem we faced at home, however, was that Nicki, now aged four, had become an early and very able reader and we were finding it difficult to stop her reading. If Dan left one of his school books lying around, Nicki would pick it up and read from it aloud. You could see the look of horror on Dan's face with the thought that his much younger sister, who hadn't even started school yet, could succeed at something he found so very difficult. Nicki would read aloud from anything and everything she could see, whether a cereal box, a toy package or an advert. This was a difficult situation to deal with, as Nicki was too young to understand the implications of her actions on Dan, and we didn't want to discourage her either. We were well aware that Nicki's early ability in reading intensified Dan's feeling of failure immensely, and asking the school for help was one of the ways we were trying to deal with this. But how wrong we were.

The whole tone of the letter indicated that our parenting skills were to blame for any difficulties Dan could be encountering. The letter even suggested that we should be doing things that we were in fact already doing, such as 'reading Dan his own bedtime story', and 'saying good morning to him in a cheery way'. And can you believe this? – it was even suggested that I tie a knot in a piece of string to keep in my pocket, and every time I felt the knot, I should remember to tell Dan that I loved him!

The letter was incredible. To me it seemed denigrating and belittling. I was devastated by it. It felt as if the school and education services were just trying to get me to back off with my requests for extra support for Dan. On the other hand, was the letter right? Were Dan's anxieties, his apparent unhappiness and his failure to thrive in the school system, the result of my poor parenting skills?

However painful the letter may have been, it was the perfect catalyst for a life-changing experience and would ultimately lead to the opening of a small independent non-fee paying school where Dan and other children could grow and thrive. This was going to be a school which would be democratically run; environmentally aware; and where parents would be completely involved and valued. Quality relationships throughout the school would be one of its main principles, and this would be key to the healthy development of every individual concerned – not just every child, but every parent too.

CHAPTER 2

How it All Began
(1966–1978)

Only in my wildest dreams as a child did I ever imagine that I would one day become a teacher. And that was the problem: I was a terrible dreamer at school, and this led to my own teachers having very low expectations for me.

One spring evening when I was ten years old, I was sitting on a cushion in the tiny porch to our house engrossed in my latest *Bunty* comic. I was waiting for my mum to return home from a school parents' evening. Hearing the sound of the gate being unfastened, I immediately looked up and smiled at my mum. But she didn't smile back. It was then that I noticed she was crying. Very concerned, I asked her what was the matter. She blurted out that my teacher, Miss Bazzly, had said, 'I'm very sorry, Mrs Mayne, but your daughter just spends all her time with her head up in the clouds and she's never going to get anywhere in life.' From that moment on, and for many years to come, I felt shame and guilt for letting my parents down. There seemed to be no question about it, Miss Bazzly had to be right: I was a lost cause; there was no hope for me.

Growing up in a small three-bedroomed semi in a suburban

area of Leeds with my parents, Alf and Vera Mayne, I was the third of four children. My mother, who still lives in the same house today, gave birth to me in the front bedroom of the family home in 1956, and to my younger sister in the same room eighteen months later. My dad was a skilled manual worker and my mum a nurse. When we were young my dad used to come in from his full-time job, have his tea, then some nights he would be out again doing part-time work at a local bar. My mum did a night shift three times a week at the local hospital. I know they struggled to make ends meet but I was one of the few in my class who didn't live on the run-down Gipton council estate where my school was situated. Not all the rooms in our house were carpeted, all our furniture had been donated by family or friends, we had no fridge or phone as some of our neighbours did, and yet I remember that, at the age of seven years, I considered we were so much better off than most of the children in my class. Looking back, my parents must have really struggled to pay the mortgage, but they were incredibly proud of the fact that they were buying their own house, and felt that by bringing their four children up in a residential area they were giving us the best possible start in life. As their children, we all carried some of that pride around with us too. Unlike some other children in my class, I was always clean and tidy, which made me feel quite special. My mother would sit up late at night making new pinafore dresses for me and my sister out of one of her own dresses. She seemed so clever. When Mum was working the night shift at the hospital, Dad was left in charge of us four children. He dutifully got us all to bed on time and either read us a story – the two girls first, and then the two boys – or told a story from memory. Me and my sister shared one room and my brothers another room. After tucking each of us up in bed he would always say, "Night night. God bless. Sweet dreams," and sometimes he would add, "Don't let the bedbugs bite!"

On the whole I had been a happy child, but something definitely changed within me, as did my parents' attitude towards me, after that fateful parents' evening. My two older brothers, Howard (three years older than me) and Ian (eighteen months older than me), and my younger sister, Julie, all passed their 11+ exam and attended grammar school. People frequently complimented my mum on the fact that she had such clever children. Without thinking, my mum would say, 'Oh yes, three of them are, but Rosalyn's a very nice girl.' That said it all, my fate was sealed. I was just a nice girl. The only future I could see was to get married young and start a family as soon as I could. There were no career expectations for me.

After failing my 11+ I had to endure five years at the local secondary modern school for girls. At the time, I felt it was rather unfortunate that my mother had placed so much emphasis on 'speaking nicely', as this made me feel very different from the majority of the girls. I had to learn some rather negative social skills pretty quickly to prevent others calling me a snob. I did my best to learn and practice Yorkshire slang, and even learned a few choice swear words in order to be accepted by my peer group.

The minimum school leaving age was fifteen in those days, and many of my friends left school at this age to find work. Somehow, though, I'd managed to work my way up from the 'B' stream to the 'A' stream, and stayed for an additional year to do a

9

few O-levels. Our class was forever being told by teachers that it was the worst exam group they'd ever had and we were unlikely to get good results. I remember quite clearly a careers lesson when one pupil asked about being a nurse and another asked about being a teacher. After sighing, the careers teacher replied that we would need an absolute minimum of five O-levels for either of these positions, which anybody in our class would find hard to achieve. It was suggested that it would be better if we looked for work in hairdressing, or in a shop, where we might get a bit of training and a certificate, or, if we worked really hard and did well in our exams, some of us might manage to get a job in a bank or building society.

It was no surprise that I left school, which had felt like a long prison sentence for a crime I couldn't remember committing, with very low self-esteem. I sat my last O-level exam and walked out of the school gates for the last time that same day. I didn't really care about my exam results, as I'd already managed to find employment. The following Monday, I started working for a small mail order company, earning £8 a week. My job consisted mainly of packing brochures into envelopes. I felt tremendous pride in being able to give my mum a small contribution towards my keep, which my 'clever' siblings were not in a position to do. A few weeks after starting the job, I received my exam results. Unbelievably, I'd actually passed all five O-levels, in English Language, English Literature, History, Domestic Science (Food) and Domestic Science (Clothing). I'd also achieved a Grade 1 CSE (Certificate in Secondary Education) – which was equivalent to another O-level in Religious Education and a Grade 2 CSE in Maths.

The mail order firm closed down shortly after I received my

results. I was then lucky enough to obtain another position, in a small private children's nursery in the Harehills area of Leeds, earning £5 a week. The lower wage didn't matter, as I'd always had a yearning to work with children. In fact I could hardly believe my luck in being paid for something I loved doing so much. I subsidised my income by working as a cashier at Tesco from 6 to 8pm on Thursdays and Fridays and all day Saturday, for which I earned an additional £2.50 a week. After a year at the Harehills-based nursery, a job which I absolutely adored, the owners decided to move on and that business too closed down.

Just before the nursery actually closed, I'd been accepted onto a full-time course combining a qualification in Child Welfare with A-levels. As I mentioned earlier, I'd had an interest in working with children for quite some time. After placing an advert in a shop window at the age of fourteen, I was inundated with offers of babysitting work, and babysat regularly for four different families. I'd completed voluntary work in a local nursery and helped to run some summer play schemes for eight to eleven year olds. At the age of sixteen I began doing voluntary work at a junior youth club on Tuesday evenings. It was while I was there that I'd started going out with Martin, who was one of the other volunteers.

Martin was five years older than me, and after seeing him for a year we did exactly what a lot of our friends were doing, and got engaged. I was only seventeen at the time, but thought I knew about life. In accordance with my teachers' expectations, it seemed an early marriage was my destiny. Martin managed to persuade me that my main priority was to save for our forthcoming marriage and our first home together rather than going to college. Besides, Martin didn't have any qualifications and he considered that he'd got a perfectly good job as a factory worker, so why should I feel the need to go to college anyway? And so it was decided that I'd turn down the college place and find work instead. This meant I was already well on the road to fulfilling the prophecy set by Miss Bazzly; a prophecy which had become absorbed by my parents and seemingly everybody else that knew me. Although my parents' love never failed, they couldn't help having low expectations for me – they were just believing what they had been told. A few of my school friends were already married and two of them already had babies. Why should I be any different?

I managed to gain full-time employment with Eagle Star Insurance as a trainee fire underwriter. This involved dealing mainly with fire and consequential loss insurance for commercial companies. After working at Eagle Star for a few weeks, I was informed by my boss that I showed enough promise to be considered for insurance exams. It was then discovered that I couldn't even start studying for these exams without O-level Maths. My CSE Grade 2 qualification was totally worthless. I can recall the Maths teacher at school telling the entire class that we were the worst Maths class ever and that we were all heading for really poor results. After such a negative attitude from her, I hadn't really seen the point in making much effort. I'm sure I could have achieved a Grade 1 (O-level equivalent) with just a little bit of encouragement.

My new boss at Eagle Star was very supportive, and the company paid for me to attend the relevant O-level Maths course at a local college. I was given some time off work on Wednesday afternoons, and also attended one evening a week in my own time. I was, however, really struggling to understand the syllabus, and the teacher wasn't much help. Mr Wroe always arrived late with a newspaper rolled under his arm. After sitting down at the front of the classroom, he would ask the class to turn to a particular page. He then instructed us to work through the exercises set, before proceeding to open his newspaper and continue with his crossword. On one occasion after putting up my hand to say I didn't understand, I eventually gained his attention, but rather than trying to explain, he responded by saying that I shouldn't be in the class then, and would probably be better off doing needlework instead! Perhaps my reply should have been that I'd already got an O-level in needlework (under the grand title of Domestic Science – Clothing) but now needed somebody to teach me Maths. He'd succeeded in humiliating me so much, however, that it stopped me from asking any further questions. This resulted in him getting back to finishing his crossword in peace, and forced me, stunned and embarrassed, to continue staring at a page of meaningless jumbled-up figures.

It seemed I'd learned nothing during my months on the O-level Maths course, and needless to say I didn't pass the exam. I later discovered that most of the other members of the class hadn't passed either. The worst thing about failing was telling my boss at Eagle Star. He was so disappointed that I found myself saying I'd take a re-sit exam at the first opportunity and assuring him that I'd make sure I passed next time!

I'd been at Eagle Star for a year and had learned a lot more about life. Also, unlike my teachers, my boss had given me a bit of positive encouragement. I believed that if I passed my O-level

Maths I could start studying for the insurance exams and might be able to have an interesting and worthwhile career after all. I had also begun to reflect on my reasons for wanting to get married. Was I just fulfilling other people's expectations of my destiny? After diligently saving for our first home as Martin had suggested, it had gradually dawned on me that I wanted the independence of having my own place more than I wanted to get married. I had been conditioned to think marriage was a means to an end, but when my friend Christine announced that she was leaving home and moving into a room in a shared house, I started to wonder what I really wanted for myself.

Subsequently, Martin and I agreed to go our separate ways, and Christine and I moved into a Victorian house in the Headingley area of Leeds. We each had our own large room, shared a kitchen between the two of us, and shared a toilet and bathroom with five other tenants. The rent was £3 a week. It was 1974, the year of the three-day week when businesses had to comply with electricity restrictions due to industrial action by the miners. I can remember having to wear extra clothes for warmth in the workplace two days a week, and on those days working fewer hours due to the lack of lighting in the office at the start and end of each day.

In an effort to pass the Maths re-sit exam, I asked my eldest brother, Howard, who was studying Chemistry at the University of Manchester, if he could help me. He agreed. For six weekends, I caught a train from Leeds to Manchester, to receive some one-to-one tuition. Unlike Mr Wroe, my brother was patient and understanding, and if I didn't understand something when it was explained one way, he would find different ways to explain it. Although it was a subject I didn't find easy, Howard just kept trying different approaches until, each time, the penny dropped and the concept would fall into place. With Howard's help and support over just six weeks, I passed the re-sit without any problems.

While visiting my brother in Manchester for help with my Maths, I got to know his live-in girlfriend, Hilary, quite well. She was a student teacher, and one day when we'd been talking about her work she suggested that I'd make a good teacher. It was difficult to take her suggestion seriously, as I still had low self-esteem, didn't have any A-levels, and, at the time of our conversation, was still struggling to get O-level Maths.

Hilary's arguments became more persuasive and encouraging. She said that in addition to the year spent working in the children's nursery, all the babysitting and voluntary work I'd done with children would go in my favour. She began to impress upon me that many colleges valued relevant experience highly. Although doubting my own capability, with Hilary's support and guidance I found myself applying for a place at teacher training college, and was absolutely stunned to find myself being accepted.

At the age of nineteen, after two years working at Eagle Star, I gave up my lovely bed-sit in Headingley and moved into halls of residence at Margaret McMillan College of Education, Bradford, to train as a nursery / first school teacher. Being classed as an independent student because I'd worked full-time for over three years, I could receive a full maintenance grant towards my education and living costs from the local education authority

(LEA). This meant that my parents didn't need to contribute anything towards my three years at college. Also, I was able to supplement my grant by returning to Eagle Star to work during the Easter and summer vacations in their Bradford office.

Initially, after starting college, what had astounded me most was the way the tutors talked to all the students. For the first time in my life, it seemed as if I was being spoken to as if I might have some intelligence. From the moment I'd failed my 11+ exam, I'd felt as if I'd been treated like a second class citizen. Now, being at college and sitting next to other students who had A-levels was an amazing, almost unbelievable experience. I remember sitting in a seminar at the start of my course and actually nipping myself hard in disbelief that I was actually there. From that point on, my self-esteem took a dramatic turn for the better.

My main subjects were Education and Sociology, and my main subsidiary subject was Drama. I enjoyed all aspects of the teaching and learning curriculum as part of the Education programme, and loved the Drama sessions. But Sociology held a certain fascination for me as it helped me to understand so many things about my own life. For example, it explained why my parents had lower expectations for me after I'd failed my 11+; why I'd felt driven to adopt negative behaviours to fit in with my peer group at secondary school; why I'd almost married at such a young age; and then why a friend leaving home to get her own place gave me the confidence to do the same.

During my three years at teacher training college, I'd grown academically, and in confidence, discovering that I wasn't as 'stupid' as my previous educators had led me to believe. For my course essays I received mainly B grades, with the occasional C and even the odd A. Not bad for someone who was told she would never get anywhere in life!

My college days were drawing to an end. Thinking ahead more and more to the days when I'd actually start teaching properly, I vowed never to make a child feel inadequate, as a number of teachers had made me feel. Reflecting upon my own school days, I realised that although Miss Bazzly's criticisms had certainly been aimed directly at me, most of the negative comments I experienced at Secondary School had been aimed at the whole class. We'd had a number of disruptive pupils in the class; I definitely wasn't one of them, but the only way the teachers felt able to respond was to shout at the whole class. It was quite soul-destroying to continually hear that you belonged to the school's worst class ever. Apart from that, there was a general acceptance that we weren't bright kids, otherwise we wouldn't be at the secondary modern anyway. Being only too aware of the long-term consequences of 'throw-away' comments that some teachers had made in my own past, I liked to think that I would never be guilty of such a crime.

On becoming a teacher, I was going to look for the positives in each individual child and build on those positives. Every child would be seen as an individual to be nurtured. I was determined that each one of them would be offered hope for the future no matter what their problem or difficulty.

My brother Howard had not only helped me to succeed where other teachers had failed, he'd also helped me to form teaching values and ideals that have stayed with me ever since. As his pupil, being gently guided and encouraged through the maze of a subject I found so difficult, I was able to experience first-hand feelings of satisfaction, almost enlightenment, as I gained in understanding. Through my brother's efforts, I came to see that my earlier attempts to pass my Maths exam were not so much my own failure as the failure of my previous teachers. Just as my brother had tried alternative approaches with regard to the O-level Maths syllabus until I understood, I'd do the same for all the pupils I would ever teach. If a child didn't understand what I was trying to teach I would regard that as my own failure, not the child's. Any difficulties would be a challenge to my teaching skills, but no matter what, I would help every individual to believe in themselves and help them to find a way to understand whatever they needed to. And so my own philosophy of education was formed, and became the foundation to my future teaching.

CHAPTER 3

Teaching
(1978-1983)

I finished college at a time when national cut-backs were being made in the number of teachers being employed. Teachers were being made redundant, and it was very hard for newly qualified teachers to obtain their first teaching posts. Initially, after qualifying, I returned to work full-time at Eagle Star in Leeds. Fortunately for me, Eagle Star had recently introduced flexi-time work, and I took advantage of these arrangements to carry out some voluntary work in a local school. I believe the fact I was doing some voluntary work helped considerably when it came to obtaining a teaching position just a few months later.

My first teaching appointment was a full-time post at an LEA nursery school in Bradford. This was a seventy-two-place nursery consisting of two classes each having their own teacher assisted by nursery nurses. Each class catered for twenty-six pupils per session, being sixteen full-time pupils aged four to five, plus twenty part-time pupils aged three to four who attended either the morning or afternoon sessions. The rooms were set out into areas for quiet or noisier activities, with large play equipment including a climbing frame, and small world toys such as a model farm, train layouts, and a dolls' house. There was a home corner; a book corner; a painting area; a water tray; a sand tray; and a large outdoor play area with a wide range of outdoor toys – it was quite typical of the majority of LEA nursery schools of the day. I loved my work at the nursery, and particularly enjoyed the singing at the end of each session. Outside school I took guitar lessons in order to accompany the children's singing, and even had a course of ten singing lessons to give me more confidence in leading the sessions, especially when parents were listening.

Teaching was fast becoming an all-degree profession. Although I had a Certificate in Education, which gave me qualified teacher status, I didn't have a degree. The Open University was becoming more and more popular as a means for teachers with the Certificate in Education to obtain a degree, and I decided that I too would take this route. It would mean many hours of part-time study in addition to teaching full-time, and as I still carried an element of self-doubt, it was a difficult decision to make. Despite becoming a teacher, the prophecy of Miss Bazzly's words telling me that I would never get anywhere in life still carried some weight.

In 1979 my sister announced her engagement to her boyfriend, Paul, who she'd been seeing for over two years. At their engagement party I met Paul's best friend, Alf Spencer. Alf and Paul had both studied Civil Engineering at Leeds University. Alf and I got on very well together and soon started seeing each other. At the time Alf was living and working in London, and I was living in Leeds, but we still managed to see each other most weekends. After a long-distance relationship for eighteen months, Alf managed to get a job in Leeds and moved into my flat. We got married three months later on 25th July 1981, just a few days before Prince Charles married Lady Diana Spencer. I was still teaching at the nursery school in Bradford at the time, and the three-year-old children who attended the nursery were particularly confused. They had been told that when they returned to nursery in September after the long summer break they would have to start calling me Mrs Spencer instead of Miss Mayne because I was getting married. Due to them also being bombarded everywhere they went by news of the royal wedding and hearing the surname Spencer every day on the news, the nursery children put two and two together and thought I was marrying Prince Charles!

I continued to teach at the nursery school in Bradford for three and a half years until I obtained a teaching position in a language centre in Bradford, teaching children, mainly of Asian origin, who spoke little or no English. I had twenty children in the class aged five to six years, and, working with a classroom assistant, we followed a structured language scheme. The children were also taught across a much broader curriculum with the emphasis on language development. This was long before the days of the National Curriculum, and we had a certain amount of freedom in how we taught. I loved teaching the children through physical activities, particularly creative movement and dance. As the language centre didn't have a hall, I spent every lunchtime moving back the furniture in my classroom to enable the children to have a movement session for their first afternoon lesson. I believed that through movement they were getting the physical benefits, of course, but also that it was a perfect medium to extend their English vocabulary in a very practical way. It helped them learn the names of different body parts; the meaning of a wide range of verbs such as running, walking, skipping, hopping, crawling; they learned the vocabulary for speed and direction – and what's more the lessons were great fun. The children loved them.

Since Alf had moved to Leeds, we'd been living in the second-floor two-bedroom flat I'd moved into as a newly qualified teacher. It was a co-ownership property, which meant that, although it was rented, after seven years the tenants started to own a percentage, which would increase year by year. I was really impressed by the scheme, thinking it was an excellent way for people to get on the housing ladder.

1981, the year we got married, was also the year of the Housing Act, which gave tenants certain rights to buy their properties. Originally I was horrified that the co-ownership philosophy was going to disappear, meaning that others couldn't benefit from such a scheme. After many sleepless nights, though, I conceded that nothing could be done to save this philosophy, so I finally agreed with Alf that we should jump on the bandwagon like everyone else.

During my second term teaching at the language centre, I was overjoyed to discover I was pregnant. As the pregnancy hormones kicked in, my emotions shifted rapidly, from the overwhelming prospect of this tiny person growing day by day inside me, to practicalities and wondering what I should do with my life after my baby was born.

I loved teaching, and it had been such a struggle for me to

get there. I also believed that I was a much better teacher than I would have been had I not experienced all those difficulties along the way. Lots of other teachers managed with child-minders during term time, and had the advantage of time with their children during the school holidays – indeed, a great perk of the job. Couldn't I do that too? No: I wanted more. I was desperate not to miss my new child growing up.

After much soul-searching, I eventually made the decision not to return to my teaching job at the language centre. I had, however, done a good deal of thinking about other options … What about having a job where I could be with my baby and could also continue teaching? … What about opening a children's nursery?

CHAPTER 4

New Beginnings
(1983-1984)

Our beautiful baby boy, Daniel Robert Spencer, was born on 3rd November, 1983. Motherhood, when it hit me, filled me with feelings of an intensity I had never thought possible. It is so true what they say, that suddenly the whole world looks a different place when you have your own baby. Even watching the TV news is a totally altered experience. As a parent you have a newly developed empathy for another whose child is missing; the child with a terminal illness; and those smitten by poverty or war. Seeing images of small children and babies starving in Ethiopia was almost unbearable. I never knew that love could be so intense, and change the way you see the world to that degree.

Within a month of Dan's birth, Alf and I managed to complete the purchase of our co-ownership flat, find a buyer almost immediately, and complete another house purchase almost simultaneously. We had bought a three-bedroom semi in the village of Sherburn-in-Elmet, not far from Leeds.

One of the things that had attracted us to our new house

when we'd first viewed it was the large brick-built detached building which had been used by the previous owner as a joiner's workshop. This was at the end of the driveway, alongside the garden. I felt that it had the potential for conversion to a children's nursery. According to Social Services regulations it would be big enough for twelve children. So the seed was planted for this idea before we purchased the house, but, being pregnant, I was more concerned about the birth of our first baby than thinking too seriously about the idea at this moment in time.

Despite the utter exhaustion of moving house combined with the lack of sleep that can come with a new baby, I was thrilled to be a new mother. As Dan grew, I played the guitar and sang to him every day while he kicked his little legs and chuckled with glee. I took him for walks in the park. I read him stories and played with him endlessly. While he slept, I studied for my Open University degree.

The weeks and months passed and even though I seemed to have everything I could ever want, there still seemed to be something missing from my life. I felt that I was losing some of the self-esteem I had gained after starting college, and the yearning to teach was as strong as ever. When Dan was five months old we decided it was time to start making plans for the opening of the children's nursery.

Being a civil engineer, Alf had no problems drawing up plans for the conversion of the outbuilding. After discussing our plans with various agencies, including the local planning department, highways, Social Services, neighbours and an adjoining landowner, we set the wheels in motion and applied for official permission to convert the outbuilding into a nursery facility for twelve children.

My first thoughts about the nursery were that it would be run on a morning-only basis so that I could enjoy the afternoons with Dan. I was really excited about the prospect of combining motherhood and teaching through running my own nursery. But one day when I phoned the planning department to check on the progress of our Change of Use application, we found that our neighbours had submitted an official objection to the plans. This was particularly upsetting because we had asked them for their views before submitting our application and they said they had no objections. When Alf came home from work on the day I'd received this news, I greeted him with tears as I explained that my dream of running the nursery had been shattered. There was still a possibility of obtaining the planning permission, but we decided that if the neighbours objected it would be too uncomfortable a prospect to go ahead. Consoling me, Alf put his arms around me and said, 'Never mind, we'll move somewhere else so that you can start a nursery!' I was extremely lucky to have such an understanding and considerate husband.

And so the search for suitable nursery premises began. We looked at numerous properties that we thought could be suitable for conversion. We were working to a very limited budget, however, so most places within our price range were either too small, had insufficient parking, or would cost too much to convert.

Our search included viewing a converted mill house not far away in Pontefract, which we considered to be absolutely perfect in every way, both as a nursery and as a home for us, even though it would have really stretched us financially. Unfortunately, though, the highways officer informed us that his department would have to recommend that the application for Change of Use to a children's nursery be refused, due to possible congestion on an adjoining road at picking-up and dropping-off time. After our last experience, I didn't know that we had the time or the money to pursue what could be another lost cause, so with great disappointment we decided to give up on what had seemed like the perfect property.

Continuing our search, we made enquiries with several estate agents. We looked at lots of different properties within our price bracket, including a derelict schoolhouse and a ramshackle pub that had lain empty for years.

Then one day, eureka! We were offered a six-bedroom detached house in Goole, overlooking the River Ouse. This was a substantial four-storey Victorian property, formerly a sea-captain's house. It had a good-sized garden, and ample parking to two sides.

Alf came with me to look at the house. There were two large reception rooms with bay windows on the upper ground floor, which was approached by a rather grand-looking flight of steps at the front. On the lower ground floor, approached by a gate at the side, were two more large rooms in addition to a large walk-in larder and a storeroom. This floor would be perfect for the two main playrooms. Two children's toilets and a staff toilet could easily be fitted into the existing larder space, and the storeroom could become an office. According to Social

Services' regulations, there was enough space to register a nursery for twenty-four children. We would have ample living space on the top two floors, where gothic-arched windows gave impressive views of the River Ouse and fields beyond. We were told that on a clear day you could see as far as Scunthorpe. We could make a decision about the upper ground floor later – perhaps we could use it as a staffroom / parents' room and storage room initially.

Alf and I both agreed that the house would be extremely suitable for our purpose, and would also be closer to his workplace at Scunthorpe than where we were living at the moment. Although badly in need of modernisation, it was situated in a desirable area of the town and the price was only £30,000. Wow!

The catch was that the top floor of the property was in a derelict state and the whole building needed a lot of work, including a new roof in the not too distant future. But we liked it, we wanted it, and thought we might be able to afford it.

Straight after the viewing, we decided to go out for a meal in Goole town centre to discuss the ins and outs of buying this particular property and generally discuss the project in more depth. We followed the signs to the town centre, but then thought we had gone wrong somewhere, as we just couldn't find it. We finished up having to ask someone. And no, we hadn't missed it. We'd just driven through it. The 'town centre' consisted of two main roads, and there didn't seem to be a restaurant on either. After asking somebody else, we were told that there was a little Indian restaurant in one of the arcades. Eventually we found the only restaurant in Goole and continued our discussions over a curry. The meal turned into a well-earned celebration, and the next day we put in an offer for the house with a view to living on the top two floors and running a children's nursery from the lower two floors.

CHAPTER 5

The Nursery
(1985-1993)

In addition to obtaining a mortgage for our new property, Alf and I would have to do some market research and prepare a business plan. Goole had a population of approximately 17,000, and seven primary schools. Only one of the schools had a nursery attached, and that had a long waiting list. There was only one other private nursery in Goole, and that did not have an educational emphasis as mine would have. There were also many surrounding villages that did not offer nursery facilities. So it looked like starting a children's nursery in Goole would be a reasonable business proposition.

Then the hard work started. Surveys, business proposals and finance needed to be sorted so that we could not only buy the property but also pay for all the necessary building alterations, nursery equipment and resources. Apart from a £6,000 deposit we would get from the sale of our house, we had no other capital. Fortunately my parents were kind enough to act as guarantors so that we could take out a business loan. We promised them that if anything went wrong with the business, Alf would go to Saudi

Arabia for a year or so to recoup any losses, as at that time civil engineers were in great demand out there.

A sale had been agreed on our three-bedroomed semi in Sherburn-in-Elmet, but unfortunately it fell through just days before the expected completion date. We had been busy promoting the opening of the new nursery in Goole and we already had some prospective clients lined up. Rather than lose our new clients, we looked at hiring alternative premises in Goole so that we could retain the interest of the parents who had already requested a place for their child.

And so, our temporary nursery opened in a church hall in January 1985. At first the numbers of children attending the nursery were low, averaging about five or six per session, but I was hoping numbers would build up gradually. From the start, I had employed a qualified nursery nurse on a full-time basis and also had a qualified teacher who just helped out for a few hours a week.

Based on the principles of educational nursery schools at the time, I'd advertised the nursery for children aged three to five years. Because Dan was so much younger than the other children attending the nursery, I knew we'd need a high staff ratio so that all the children's needs could be adequately met. Dan enjoyed the attention of the older nursery children, who were more than happy to amuse him, and whenever possible I would spend my lunch break with him.

The sale of our house in Sherburn-in-Elmet and the purchase of our four-storey house in Goole, with its beautiful gothic windows and river views, eventually took place in February 1985. There were then several weeks of hard work, carried out mainly by Alf, with lots of help from his dad and a few local workmen, before the new nursery was eventually ready. Victoria House Nursery School, as we decided to call it, opened in April 1985. So my dream had become reality, thanks to my parents acting as guarantors and the hard work carried out mainly by Alf and his dad.

'Living above the shop' was not all plain sailing. It was hard work but, like lots of things in life, there were both positives and negatives. On the down side, Dan had to share me, and I was not always immediately available to meet his needs as his mother because of my responsibility to the other children. The benefits, however, were tremendous. Dan learned to share at an early age. And even though he didn't always have his mother meeting his personal needs, he got to know certain members of staff very well, and they shared the responsibility for his care. He enjoyed many different activities with children who became his good friends.

As I was my own boss, I arranged my working hours so that I could spend Tuesday and Thursday afternoons on my own with Dan. These were our 'special afternoons' and we would spend them baking together, going for a walk, visiting Grandma and Grandad in Leeds, going shopping, watching a video, playing games, or some other special activity. We both looked forward to these times together.

A great perk of living above the nursery was that I could postpone many typical teaching duties until later in the evening so that I could spend the early part of the evening upstairs with Dan. We'd be together for his mealtime, bathtime and bedtime story. When he was fast asleep and Alf was home from work to keep an eye on him, I would often go downstairs again to do some display work or other jobs that needed doing in the nursery.

As Dan grew older, we changed and adapted. The nursery continued to thrive and Dan seemed to love being part of it. We had built up some excellent resources and a good team of staff. A Special School just around the corner from the nursery allowed us to use their swimming pool once a week; we also used their large hall for our gym and movement lessons. Dan enjoyed his experience of being in the nursery, and everybody knew him as a happy and confident child.

Over the years the nursery built an excellent reputation. Most of the parents brought their children to the nursery based on personal recommendations. We had worked hard at building our respected reputation with the local schools, and always liaised closely with their future teachers when children transferred from us to primary school. A number of local headteachers even sent their staff to our nursery for training days because of our good practice.

From the very first day of the opening of my nursery I held parents in the highest regard. I had always believed that the best way to help a child was to work closely with the parents. In my first teaching job at the LEA nursery school in Bradford, I had instigated home visits, which I carried out in my own time in my lunch breaks and after school. Prior to the opening of the nursery, I visited all the families in their own homes. I valued every parent's opinion, and welcomed the opportunity to deal effectively with any concerns they might have had. Whenever a new child joined the nursery, I always encouraged the parent to stay with their child for all of the first session, and then only start to leave them for short periods of time. For the next two or three sessions, many parents would make use of our comfortable parents' room so that they were close by if their child was finding the separation difficult. I liked this gradual start to nursery life whereby the child could begin to feel safe and secure in their new environment and confident that their parent was going to return. We did our best to nurture both the child and the parent.

Many parents were more than willing to assist with special activities such as the weekly swimming sessions and any trips and outings. A parents' group was set up that had a say in certain aspects of the running of the nursery and also as a social group. I held regular parents' evenings, suggesting ways parents could help their children learn at home, and explaining the reasoning behind many of the activities in the nursery. I also offered individual consultations with parents so that we could share useful information about their child.

Even though we fed about fourteen different schools, including some in outlying villages, I always made a point of meeting with each child's new class teacher because I believed it would ease the transition for the children as well as building good relationships with the schools. I also found this an invaluable experience for keeping up to date with what was happening in local schools and knowing what groundwork future teachers would like me to be covering with their prospective pupils. If I was teaching a child how to write their name, for example, I would ensure that we would use the lettering style of the school they would be joining, since there could be variations from school to school.

The quality of my staff was of upmost importance. I always employed a qualified teacher in addition to myself, to give me some time to deal with any other issues that required my attention, or in the cases when I was attending training myself, or visiting other schools, or if Dan was poorly. Initially there was always a teacher in attendance for five full days each week, but as time went on we restructured the sessions and the fees so that a teacher was only in attendance during the 'Educational' morning sessions. We charged slightly more for these sessions to cover the cost of the teacher. In order to make the fees more affordable to less well off families, we offered structured play sessions in the afternoon led by a qualified nursery nurse. It wasn't very long after the nursery opened that we started to offer after-school clubs and school holiday care facilities for children aged up to eight years.

Through knowledge I gained at training conferences and numerous early years events, I cascaded as much training as I could to my staff personally (in order to keep costs down). I also bought in course materials that we would run through together. One was an Open University Early Years course; another, a National Children's Bureau course. On occasion I bought in external trainers and sold places to early-years workers from other organisations to help contribute towards the costs. An event I took advantage of every year was a visit over one or two days to the three-day Education Show at the National Exhibition Centre in Birmingham. At this event, I would attend as many free training seminars as possible, as well as gleaning up-to-date information and buying new resources for the nursery from the hundreds of exhibiting stalls at the event. On some occasions, other members of the nursery staff would give up a Saturday to come with me because they too found it such a valuable experience.

Dan started school in the second week of September 1988, and just a few days later, on Monday 12th September, his sister Nichola Anne Spencer (Nicki) was born. In preparation for the birth and the following months, and to help me settle Dan into school, Helen Chase, who had been teaching at the nursery part-time for a number of years, took over my teaching role for a term.

By now the nursery had developed considerably. Due to endless requests from parents to provide not only education facilities for three to five year olds but also care for younger children, we had introduced separate facilities for babies and toddlers. Initially when I returned to teaching the term after Nicki's birth, I made use of these facilities myself, and Nicki always seemed content and well cared for. We had a superb team in the baby room, and Nicki formed a special attachment with nursery assistant Joanne Rhodes.

By the time Nicki was two, we had improved our facilities even more and moved the facilities for babies and toddlers into a five-room annexe which we rented from the adjoining building. The Babes 'n' Tots Annexe, as we called it, which was managed by qualified and experienced nursery nurses, specialised in caring for children up to the age of two and a half to three years, depending on individual development. It had a messy playroom, a large 'jungle' playroom, a sleep room, a bathroom with purpose-built facilities, and a kitchen. We were registered for a maximum of twelve babies and toddlers in the Annexe.

The upper ground floor of the main building had also been extended and converted so that it had a large room for educational group activities plus a Rumpus Room consisting of large soft play equipment, a climbing frame and a slide. We were now registered for a total of thirty-four children in the main building and twelve in the Annexe, giving a total of forty-six.

Only a limited number of children required full-time care; the majority of older nursery children attended the morning educational sessions, and some just attended two play sessions a week.

In the summer term of 1993, after a full day's independent inspection by an early years' researcher, we were given an excellent write-up in the first edition of the *Good Nursery Guide*. The researcher's closing comments were: '*An interesting and well-equipped nursery and nursery school, where every child is special.*'

Some people mistakenly thought that I made a lot of money out of the nursery. Unfortunately this wasn't true; perhaps my standards were too high. We were usually overstaffed and never understaffed – that was something I was always really careful about. In addition to the nursery staff employed to look after the children, I employed a cook, an administrator and a cleaner. I employed additional staff over lunch times and even for preparation of drinks and snacks so that there was always the full quota of staff to children. Years later, while working as an Ofsted-registered nursery inspector, I found that this practice was quite unusual. In addition to many private nurseries that 'doubled up' the child:adult ratio during staff breaks, I found that most local authority nurseries did this too. No wonder I didn't seem to be making much money.

Out of nursery hours, Alf and I made sure we spent as much quality time as possible with our own children. After Nicki's birth, I had an endowment policy mature, and we used the money to make part-payment on a static caravan at Filey, near Scarborough. Although we needed to let the caravan out for part of the year to cover the repayments, ground rent costs and other expenses, we spent as many weekends as we could there, in addition to full weeks 'out of season' (when we were less likely to get bookings). I can recall many hours spent making sandcastles on the beach, paddling in the sea, cycling and walking (initially with Nicki in a baby seat or child carrier). Dan loved having rides on the steam trains of the North Yorkshire Railway, making dens with his friends in nearby woodland, playing with his remote-controlled car, and sitting round the table with jigsaws or playing cards.

As family life went on and Dan continued to struggle at school, I reflected again and again on the letter from the educational psychologist. Was I a bad parent? I really had done my best to ensure that Dan was happy and well cared for. His needs were forever upmost in my mind. Was there any justification for the apparent criticism of my parenting skills? Should I not have started the nursery? Should I have spent more time with Dan? But doesn't every mother who works ask these same questions? It needs to be remembered that there is no perfect solution and there is no such thing as a perfect parent. When your child is struggling, it is easy to blame yourself. Even more so when you feel that the professionals are pointing the finger at you.

CHAPTER 6

Growing Concerns
(1988–1992)

Dan's personality had begun to change after he'd started school. He had often been tired and down-hearted when I'd collected him. I had to take into account that he not only had to deal with the new demands of full-time schooling but also had to adjust to a new baby in the home and the fact that he was no longer an only child. We gave him as much love and reassurance as we could when he came home from school, and he enjoyed helping with the new baby. Although I was breast-feeding Nicki, I would supplement this with a bottle so that Dan could, if he wanted to, hold her on his knee and feed her. Under the circumstances I think we did the best we could so that Dan didn't feel pushed out.

Time progressed and Dan didn't seem any happier. Over the next few years any comments I made to the school about possible dyslexia were quickly dismissed, and generally sharing our concerns with his teachers often left me feeling very frustrated.

On one occasion I suggested to the school that Dan might find it easier to work using the computer rather than writing by hand, which he found so very difficult. The teacher didn't like this idea, even though I believe to this day that it could have helped him.

Dan loved anything mathematical and there had been a time when Dan said the only thing he really liked at school was numeracy. He was devastated when he reached the stage when his number work started to take a written-sentence format. He just couldn't deal with the problems presented in this way.

At an open evening at the school I explained to the teacher that Dan was having great difficulty understanding the written maths questions. She replied that Dan simply had to ask her to read the question for him. I know that she was trying to be helpful and meant well, but Dan could work out the answers so fast once he knew the question that he would be ready for the next question to be read out almost immediately. Having thirty children in the class plying for her attention would mean that she couldn't meet Dan's needs in this respect, so Dan felt like a failure in the only subject he thought he was good at.

One weekend we were all staying as a family at our caravan at Filey. Dan was about seven at the time. On the Sunday afternoon we were playing on the beach when I noticed that something was bothering Dan. It turned out he was worrying about the spelling test at school the following day. In an effort to help him, I made a game of writing the words he needed to learn for the test using a stick to form the letters in the sand. Eventually Dan could write the words in the sand on his own, and seemed more relaxed and confident. We were then able to get on with the more enjoyable task of building sandcastles. Back at our caravan a short while later, however, Dan couldn't remember any of the spellings.

Previously, as a co-opted governor at Dan's school, I had arranged to spend a morning looking around the whole school with a view to reporting back at the next governors' meeting. I spent some time in the combined Reception and Year One class where Dan was at the time. Also in the class were a number of children who I knew very well because they had attended my own nursery and I had been directly involved in teaching them.

My heart started aching for one particular ex-pupil of mine that morning as she spent over an hour trying to copy a sentence from the blackboard into her book. Jenny was an August baby and she had only just had her fourth birthday the week before she started school, whereas Dan was nearly five when he started. That one-year age span is absolutely tremendous when you are only four years old. In the nursery, Jenny had loved painting and craft activities, and socialising with other children in the home corner. She had loved books, and was able to read some simple words on her own. She had started to develop her writing skills nicely before she left the nursery, and was able to write her name independently as well as copying some simple words like 'mummy' or 'daddy' to accompany her pictures.

The morning of my visit to school, however, Jenny seemed a completely different child. She was sitting at her table looking utterly hopeless as she struggled to copy the string of meaningless letter shapes forming a sentence into her work book. She had not finished the task by playtime, so was asked to complete it after play. She looked desperately unhappy because she was aware that most of the other children had completed the task long ago and had moved on to more interesting practical activities. It was as though she were being punished for being younger than the other children. In my opinion, she was not yet ready for such a task even though she was a very bright child.

Just like my son, I could see that Jenny was experiencing the pain of failure. I need to add that the teacher was doing the best she could under the circumstances. I was aware that she had originally been trained to teach older primary children but was now teaching a mixed-age group of Reception and Year One children aged four to six. As far as I was aware she hadn't much experience of early years teaching but she carried the reputation of being an excellent teacher. That day, she had set the children the initial task of writing up the news for the day, and once they had finished this task they could move on to some really exciting and stimulating activities. I loved the way she'd wrapped up parcels of different sizes and shapes to make her post-office activity more interesting for the children. She'd incorporated numeracy and literacy activities in a fun way. It was just unfortunate that amongst all the exciting and fun activities going on, which I couldn't fault, she hadn't noticed poor Jenny struggling. I really don't think the teacher had taken into account that if Jenny had been born just a week later, she'd still be in a nursery class where she wouldn't have had to spend over an hour grappling with an almost impossible task – she'd be having fun and learning through play.

One week when Dan had been off school with chickenpox, I took time off from teaching in the nursery to be with him. I really enjoyed sitting down with him and helping him with his schoolwork. Dan was incredibly responsive to my input. It really was so much easier than trying to offer him help at the end of the school day when he was tired and irritable.

Having had such positive learning experiences with Dan at home during his illness, I wondered if I would be allowed to withdraw Dan from school one afternoon a week in order to carry out that valuable one-to-one time with him again. I already tried to keep Tuesday and Thursday afternoons free, and left somebody else in charge of the nursery, so that I could give Nicki some quality time (the way I had done with Dan). The school promptly said no to my suggestion: under no circumstances could they allow me to educate Dan off site during school time. It was actually perfectly legal for this to happen and for the school to use a specific symbol in the school register to indicate the child was being educated off site. It would not have affected the school's funding in any way at all. Unfortunately though, not many schools would do this even though it would have been of benefit to the child. Dan's headteacher suggested that as an alternative I could go into school for an afternoon each week, but would have to work with a group of children, not just Dan. I said that I'd be more than happy to do this. Unfortunately this never happened; after thinking about it, the school recalled that they had a policy of not letting parents work with their own children in school. They said that I could go into school and work with a group of other children though!

A few weeks later when I was taking Dan and Nicki swimming, Dan pointed to a lady in the car park and said, 'That's the lady that does special work with me at school!'

'Oh, that's nice,' I replied, concealing my concern that the school had not informed me of this. 'What do you do when you see her?'

'We play some spelling games and things,' said Dan.

'Do you enjoy that?' I asked him.

'Yes, it's all right, but I always have to miss apparatus work though!' he replied with disappointment in his voice.

Dan was a clumsy child who struggled to participate in school sports days and never wanted to play football. I was concerned that he was missing a lesson he really enjoyed, one that might help him to improve the coordination skills he lacked.

I arranged another meeting at the school and explained how appreciative I was of Dan receiving special help but that I was concerned about him missing a lesson that he not only really enjoyed, but could help him with something else he found difficult. The headteacher responded with an exasperated, 'Well, what DO you want, Mrs Spencer!' I was quite certain I hadn't been confrontational in my manner, but I went away feeling like an awkward and fussy parent. Instead of trying to work out what was best for Dan, they had become automatically defensive. In the past, I had felt I had enjoyed a very good relationship with the school, but now I felt very uncomfortable, and I believed that continuing to discuss Dan's problems with them might make things worse.

I didn't know it at the time, but looking back I think that in addition to being dyslexic, Dan could also have been dyspraxic. Dyspraxia is a condition that affects physical coordination skills. This could explain why Dan appeared clumsy at times and found some sports activities so difficult.

As time passed, I wasn't just concerned about Dan but other children who had attended my nursery too. While I was delighted that some parents were able to give me very positive feedback, saying that the nursery had prepared their child well for school and they had settled in happily and were making good progress, I was concerned about the number of parents whose children were experiencing problems. Some children who were settled and happy while attending the nursery, perhaps on a part-time basis, were now showing sign of stress at having to attend school full time. Some of the children had become so anxious that they had started to wet their beds, whereas they had been dry at night before starting school. Other children didn't want to go to school for a variety of reasons and were encountering different problems. It seemed, then, that Dan wasn't the only child to lose his sparkle upon starting school.

Interestingly, some of the parents had very similar stories to my own, in that suggestions had been made about their parenting ability when they had sought further support for their child in school.

By now Dan's sister, Nicki, was four years old and had just missed going to school with all her friends from the nursery because she'd been born twelve days too late. Although Jenny, whom I'd observed years before in Dan's class, had been the youngest in her class and hadn't been ready for some of the activities she had been asked to tackle, Nicki would probably be the oldest child in her year group. This fact, combined with the knowledge that Nicki was already an avid reader and writer, gave me other concerns ...

Some of the parents whose children had attended the nursery had relayed stories about their very able children being held back in Reception class and having to wait for the other children to 'catch up'. Springing immediately to mind are three children who were all confident early readers when they left the nursery but who all had difficulty in Reception. One was made to start again at Book One, a process he found so humiliating and degrading that it turned him off books even though he'd been a very enthusiastic reader up to that point. Another boy was not allowed to take a reading book home at all for his entire first year at school. He too found this a demoralising experience. Another very able child had her reading restricted, resulting in her too losing her enthusiasm for books.

Nicki was the opposite of Dan when it came to reading and writing. I would have had no worries about her going to school twelve months earlier, when all her friends started – she was ready. If she'd been born two weeks sooner, I feel that she would have been with the appropriate age group for her ability and level of maturity. But now didn't seem to be the right time for her to start with a typical Reception group, and I feared that school would dampen her enthusiasm for learning too.

So like lots of other parents, I now had anxieties about both of my children and was wondering how the education system could possibly meet their very individual needs. On top of this, I had concerns about some of the children who had left the nursery and were now struggling due to learning difficulties, able children being held back, or coping with other difficulties such as bullying.

In September 1992, when Dan was two months away from his ninth birthday and Nicki had just had her fourth birthday, I was still wondering how I could help them both when I received a newsletter from Human Scale Education (HSE). I didn't know very much about the organisation at the time but think I may have expressed an interest in their philosophy while visiting a stand at the Education Show at the NEC in Birmingham the previous year. The headlines of the newsletter read: *THE WHITE PAPER – Hope for small schools at last?* The article by Satish Kumar referred to the government white paper *Choice and Diversity* published in July 1992. It suggested that Britain could see the development of more diverse schools that would offer parents much more variety and choice. I read the following paragraph over and over again:

> *If these are not empty promises, we may see the emergence of Danish-style schools, founded by parents. New small schools, as well as Muslim and Christian schools may achieve the same status as grant-maintained schools. If so, and this is a big 'if', then all the effort put into producing this White Paper may be worthwhile.*

This newsletter prompted me to reread an earlier HSE Newsletter which showed the organisation's patrons on the front page. I found myself looking at photographs of the patrons and immediately recognised the familiar and friendly face of Anita Roddick of the highly successful Body Shop chain. She had been a teacher but had become disillusioned and had felt she could help more people through producing fair-trade products in an environmentally caring way. Other patrons included Sir Yehudi Menuhin, the incredibly gifted musician who as a child had been educated at home; Jonathan Porritt, a public figure associated with environmental issues (and a good friend of Prince Charles); Lord Young of Dartington, the brainchild behind the Open University; Professor Tim Brighouse, and Professor Richard Pring. The overall message given by the patrons in the newsletter was that education in Britain was in crisis. The then Secretary of State for Education, Kenneth Clark, was arguing that progressive education had failed our children, and was talking about schools *getting back to basics*. The aforementioned patrons feared the consequences of Kenneth Clark's policies and wanted to see education become more child-centred. Jonathan Porritt stated: *'The education system today is largely out of touch with the real world, not just in terms of curriculum content but of practice and process. Human Scale Education is an important part of redressing that balance.'*

Inspired by everything I had read, I picked up the phone and rang HSE. It was a phone call that was to change not only my own life but Dan's, Nicki's and others' too …

CHAPTER 7

Finding a Better Way
(November 1992)

A few weeks later I was on my way to London to attend a two-day residential workshop entitled 'How to Set Up a Small School'. Following an early start to the day, I arrived by train at Kings Cross station and walked to the Friends' Meeting House where the workshop was due to take place.

On my arrival I was led upstairs to a small, clean, comfortable single room, and shown the shared bathroom facilities. After spending a few minutes on my own putting some of my belongings in the drawers and gathering my thoughts, I decided with great apprehension to make my way downstairs to the meeting room.

I was the first participant to arrive, and was greeted warmly by the coordinator of Human Scale Education, Fiona Carnie, who I'd already spoken to on the phone. I was beginning to feel as if I already knew her, which helped to put me considerably more at ease. A few minutes later I was being introduced to Colin Hodgetts, whose appearance at first reminded me of Terry Waite, but then his smiling eyes and the great warmth he exuded made me liken him more to, dare I say, Santa Claus. I was informed that Colin was the headteacher at The Small School, in Hartland, Devon, had been for the past nine years, and was going to be leading the workshop.

Fiona showed me to the kitchen area, and as I was making a drink other people started to arrive. Their smiles and friendly faces soon reassured me that I was going to enjoy getting to know everybody over the weekend. After a few minutes of chatting in the tiny kitchen, Fiona asked us if we'd like to come through and we'd get started.

The beige-carpeted meeting room, with its pale green walls, was comfortably furnished with a selection of easy chairs. The surroundings were simple, reflecting the Quaker principles on which every Friends' Meeting House is based. In addition to Colin, Fiona and myself, there were seven other people attending the workshop. The ten of us only just managed to fit into the room, which made the gathering feel intimate and somehow more meaningful. Listening with great interest to Colin, we all heard the story of how The Small School in Hartland was set up. The founder of The Small School was Satish Kumar, the writer of the article that led to me phoning Human Scale Education in the first place. Satish was also the editor of *Resurgence Magazine*. Formerly a Jain monk, he had moved to Hartland, Devon, with his wife June and their two young children. While their son and daughter were attending the local primary school, Satish and his wife had no real concerns about their education. But when their son, Mukti, was approaching the end of his primary schooling, Satish became concerned about him travelling a great distance to attend the closest secondary school in a neighbouring town.

He believed that not only was the school too large and impersonal but there were numerous issues involved in taking young people out of the community where they have grown up and transporting them a considerable distance. He also questioned the value of mass secondary education, peer group pressure, materialistic values, and such a strong emphasis on examinations. He wanted a more spiritual, holistic education, not only for his own two children, but for other secondary-age pupils in Hartland too.

Satish was so enthusiastic about his educational vision for Hartland, that when a former chapel came up for sale at auction in 1982 he bid £20,000 in order to purchase the building to set up The Small School. He had borrowed the deposit from *Resurgence* and in the next issue of the magazine appealed to the readers to buy £2,000 worth of shares in the building, and the £20,000 was promptly raised.

Colin went on to tell us that the first year of the school didn't run smoothly and there were great differences in educational philosophy between Satish and the school's former headteacher. Satish then approached Colin, whom he had worked with in the past setting up a 'non-violent' project in London, and from whom he had also sought advice in the setting up of The Small School. Colin, a teacher and Church of England clergyman, subsequently took over as the head's replacement in September 1983.

Colin explained the philosophy of the school in meeting the needs of four groups: parents; the rural community; teachers; and pupils. An extract from his new publication gave a little more background:

The school teaches the National Curriculum but within a commitment to the development of the whole person, body, mind and spirit, in all its aspects, creative, practical, intellectual, ethical and emotional.

Just as there is an emphasis on the development of the whole person so also is there a concern to explore the interconnections between subjects and to see humankind as interdependent with the natural world.

The person of the teacher is more important than the matter taught or the methods used … The spirit of the place is that of family. Not any family: a disciplined one in which there is mutual respect.'

'Inventing a School: The Small School, Hartland', by Colin Hodgetts (page 30)

The number of secondary pupils at The Small School had fluctuated between thirty-three and thirty-six, aged eleven to sixteen years. The essential admissions criteria was that pupils must live in, or very close to, Hartland. Although they got a lot of enquiries from parents willing to move to the area (from as far afield as Scotland) just so that their children could attend the school, they discouraged this because they felt it put unrealistic pressures on the school.

During the weekend workshop, Colin also explained that Human Scale Education was set up by a group who met at Dartington to discuss education. Many people had been contacting The Small School for help and advice, and it was thought that by setting up HSE as a separate entity, it could not only respond to these queries but also help to make its philosophy more widely known, and hopefully inspire others to follow in the path of The Small School. Hence the reasoning behind us all being there that weekend.

Over the weekend we looked at the difficulties of finding suitable premises and other practicalities of starting a school. These included the requirements of the Department for Education regulations, essential equipment needed, the National Curriculum, and whether to set up as a limited company, a charitable trust or a cooperative. We learned about the philosophy and principles of HSE and the organisation's belief that education should be free and available to all. The charging of fees was strongly opposed. This led on to a discussion of the financial side of setting up a school. We looked at basic running costs, and ways of obtaining trust funding and/or charitable donations to meet some of these costs.

As the workshop progressed, I was starting to get to know more about the other people in the group and why they had wanted to attend the weekend. One of the participants was a creative dance teacher who believed in a more spiritual approach to education and would have liked to work in a small school. Another participant, Kevin Fossey, was at that time the headteacher of a 450-place state primary school in Brighton. He was very unhappy with the principles of state education at the time, and as a practising Buddhist he wanted to be involved in setting up the first Buddhist school in Britain. Kevin Holloway was Head of Mathematics Education at Bretton Hall College of Education. He had concerns for his own two children in the state system and wanted to find out more about the possibilities of a group of people setting up a small school. Another participant had a story almost identical to my own. Her name was Jane and, like me, she was already running a children's nursery and had worries for her own son as well as having concerns about the future for some of her nursery children. Her husband, who taught Physical Education in a state secondary school, was there to support her and to see how he could be involved in the setting up of a small school. There were also two women there who had just set up a small school in Poole, Dorset.

Because the group was such a small one compared to many other training events I have attended, and perhaps in keeping with the philosophy of HSE, comfortable relationships were beginning to develop between members of the group. And something else was also developing in me: a belief that if The Small School had started off with nothing and had done so well, then surely others could too.

Kevin Holloway wanted to know a lot more about the financial aspects. How could these schools survive if they were not fee-paying schools? In particular, how much could the teachers be paid? Colin talked about how the school had initially received a substantial amount of funding from the Gulbenkian Foundation, and then from other trusts. Fund-raising was a continuing effort and Colin tried to spend one day a week purely writing letters to charitable trusts and trying to access other sources of funding. The teachers all helped the cause by receiving a low salary. As headteacher of the school, Colin received £8,000 a year. In fact, he explained, all the full-time staff got paid the same: the caretaker, the cook, the other teachers.

Kevin Fossey was aware that the teachers at The Small School in Hartland were lowly paid but still wanted to see a day when he could relinquish his current headship and become involved in setting up the country's first Buddhist primary school (something he achieved a few years later).

Kevin Holloway, on the other hand, was much more sceptical. He felt that the teachers' wages were inadequate. In response, Colin Hodgetts replied that the low wages were a means of survival for the school, but he hoped in some ways that things would improve. He believed that if more people opened small schools on a similar basis to The Small School in Hartland, then the government might eventually take notice. He was very hopeful that the government's White Paper proposing more choice for parents would become reality and result in parent-run schools being state funded in Britain, as they are in Denmark and Holland.

In further defence of the low wages for the teaching staff, Colin said that he believed that the world had become too materialistic and that many of the values children are exposed to in state schools promote a materialistic society. He said that he and the other staff had learned to manage on the smaller salary. Living 'a simpler life' has many benefits for the individual and to society. Colin explained how he and his partner, Julia (who also teaches at The Small School) economise with heating and other forms of energy they use, always use fresh food as opposed to expensive pre-packaged food, are happy to use charity shops for clothes, and will repair items rather than replace them unless absolutely necessary. Their entire way of life is low-cost in monetary terms, not materialistic, and environmentally friendly. He felt the emotional rewards were tremendous.

Reflecting on my own school days again, I remembered a teacher telling us that the reason for us going to school was so that we could pass exams in order to obtain higher-paid jobs, enabling us 'to own bigger houses and better cars' than those who didn't work hard at school! The philosophy of The Small School could not have been more different.

We all found it very interesting to learn that the pupils were actually discouraged from taking more than five GCSEs (although these must include English and Maths). The school encourages a more rounded approach to education and life skills, and aims to produce young adults who are capable of far more than just passing exams. All the pupils take part in practical activities such as organic gardening, planning and preparing the school meals, building work (the pupils had recently built a new chemistry lab for the school) and other crafts. The pupils also have time to discuss environmental values and hold democratic meetings about the running of the school. Colin confidently stated that nobody needed more than five GCSEs at A to C grade, and these were normally sufficient to enable students to attend a college of further education to study A-levels if they so wished. He also commented on the fact that universities such as Oxford and Cambridge were keen to have ex-pupils of The Small School because they tended to demonstrate an unusual openness of mind, a willingness to learn, an aptitude to apply themselves and a certain maturity that many others of their age didn't possess. Overall, Colin believed that the academic children at his school were more rounded than they would have been had they been crammed with exam material, and he also believed that the non-academic children performed much better in their exams than they would have done in a results-based environment.

In the majority of schools, success is measured in academic terms and the pupils who know that they are not so academic are more likely to feel inadequate in comparison to other pupils. In some schools this is known to lead to disaffection among the pupils considered less able. At The Small School in Hartland there is more equality between the academic and not so academic pupils, and practical skills are seen to be as valuable as academic skills. It is felt that because the less academic have the same status within the school as the academic pupils, they have greater self-esteem and consequently perform better in exams than they may have done otherwise. Likewise, the more academic pupils are able to cook and carry out practical tasks with confidence, and they have genuine respect for people who choose practical tasks for a living. This is the same philosophy as that professed by Mohandas Gandhi (1869–1948), the Indian nationalist leader known by his followers as Mahatma, which means 'Great Soul'.

We also learned about the special mealtimes at The Small School. The pupils were directly responsible for planning, preparing and serving the daily vegetarian lunch. Every pupil in the school had their turn, working in pairs, assisted by a teacher who worked with them in the school kitchen. The

Principles of Human Scale Education

1. Education should be a life-long process, involving a development of the whole person, intellectual, moral, physical, with a wide range of ideas, attitudes, skills and information.

2. Each person is a member of several communities, from his or her family to the community of the whole earth, with rights, responsibilities and obligations; human scale education relationships are founded on mutual respect and care for others and the environment.

3. In human scale education each person is valued equally and achievement is broadly defined and celebrated; expectations should be high and each person should be able to succeed.

4. Learning should be an active process, where learners become aware of their own development and identify for themselves how to extend their range of understanding. Teaching should be a helping activity, not a delivery system for packaged knowledge.

5. Education should be a partnership – between learner and teacher, learner and community, teacher and parent and between learners themselves.

6. Access to education should not be artificially predetermined by previous experience or lack if it.

7. All people should have a right to education on a human scale.

WHY A HUMAN SCALE EDUCATION MOVEMENT?

The principles outlined above, many of which are generally accepted by most people in education, cannot be implemented within the framework of the existing education system. A profound reconstruction is needed along human scale lines to provide a framework in which learners and teachers can know each other, feel secure and belong. Such a framework would include structures and environments which are nurturing and stimulating. Also it should recognise the rights and responsibilities, in partnership, of parents, students and teachers, treating all those involved as whole people with present rights and future needs. In general, their interests both as individuals and as members of a social group are best served by open access and equal entitlement to a varied curriculum. Where there are schools, these should be common schools for all children providing maximum partnership with parents. We accept that families should retain the right to educate their children at home, and believe that this should also be possible in partnership with schools. We see the benefits of an educational framework based on human scale principles as providing:

a) Better relationships in schools, with a more natural integration of education and welfare.
b) The encouragement of an active style of learning, and increased group and independent learning.
c) Greater individuality in the content and pace of learning.
d) A more natural environment in which to learn social responsibility.
e) Greater involvement of pupils with parents, other adults and the community.
f) Greater opportunity for encouraging self-discipline and building up self-confidence, self-reliance and capability.

* Handout received during the 'How to Set Up a Small School' Workshop

school had its own vegetable garden and close links with the village shop. Not only did this process cover so many areas of the curriculum in an experiential and very practical way, but the children gained invaluable life skills. The kitchen was regarded as the heart of the school, and any pupils experiencing difficulties in the classroom, or any other problem, would be welcome in the kitchen, a place where they could always find solace. The lunchtime meal itself was regarded as a very important part of the school day, when staff and children would sit together at carefully set tables. Following a moment's silence after The Peace Prayer (composed by Satish Kumar), they would all enjoy the two course 'home-made' meal and partake in pleasant conversation amongst staff and pupils together.

As the workshop progressed, I felt a sense of enlightenment. Colin's most used word seemed to be 'vision', and that was exactly what I was beginning to develop. In addition to the apprehension I felt, there was an almost overwhelming excitement in the pit of my stomach. Everything I was hearing from Colin was music to my ears. I couldn't wait to become one of his disciples and set up a small school with a similar philosophy in North Humberside (later to become East Yorkshire).

Over the weekend I had become quite friendly with Kevin Holloway. He was the only other person on the course who was from the north of England. Although he worked at Bretton Hall College of Education near Wakefield, the home of the Yorkshire Sculpture Park, he lived in Bradford, which was of course where I had trained and taught. Over coffee breaks and meals I reminisced about Bradford with Kevin. On one occasion Kevin and I were having a lengthy chat about our personal educational experiences. Like me, Kevin had failed his 11+ exam, yet here he was years later with a Masters degree and Head of Maths Education at Bretton Hall. Kevin told me how, after failing his 11+, he spent four years at a typical secondary modern school that had low expectations for most of the pupils. Due to a family relocation, however, he moved to a boys' comprehensive school to complete his secondary education. This school generally had higher expectations for its pupils, and the teaching was much more focused. Kevin had less than a year at this school before sitting his O-levels, so he did very well to achieve four. Although pupils normally needed to have at least five O-levels to move up to the Sixth Form, the teachers at this school had spotted that Kevin had potential and allowed him to stay on. Over the next two years, he managed to complete another three O-levels plus three good A-levels, which led to him receiving offers for a university place. I wondered what his future would have looked like had he remained at the secondary modern? It would definitely have been harder for him to get to where he was in his career at that moment in time, and his life chances would probably have been very different.

Having chatted about our personal experiences, Kevin and I both expressed concerns for our children's lifetime opportunities based on what we believed to be inadequacies within the state education system. Telling me about his daughter, Laura, Kevin explained how she used to love school but her school experiences relating to the SATs (in those days standing for Standard Assessment Tasks rather than 'Tests') were now causing her some distress. She found that her teacher was no longer available to offer help and advice because she was carrying out assessments and couldn't be disturbed. Additionally, Kevin's son, Matthew, was also having problems conforming to petty rules and regulations at his school. Overall, Kevin had grave concerns about mainstream schooling. He told me that as well as being a member of HSE, he was also a member of an organisation called Education Now, which was campaigning for changes to be made to the education system.

As the two-day workshop came to an end, we all bid each other goodbye. Some, like me, were bubbling with enthusiasm to go away and start something similar to The Small School in Hartland. Others, like Kevin Holloway, went away duly impressed but a bit more sceptical. As Kevin was also heading for Kings Cross station, we walked there together talking about the weekend all the way, until parting to catch our different trains.

The train journey from London to Goole that evening was one I shall never forget. I couldn't stop writing in my notebook, one idea after another. By the end of the journey I had pages of notes relating to plans for a small school. I had also drafted a design for a flyer that I could send out to all my nursery parents inviting them to attend a public meeting regarding the possibility of setting up a small school in the town of Goole.

Returning home tired but elated, I discussed the weekend with Alf. I don't think he was very sure about the idea of trying to get a small school started, but he could see I was utterly convinced that it was the best thing we could do for Dan and

Nicki, especially Dan, not to mention the other ex-nursery pupils I was so concerned about. Although Alf had reservations, particularly about the financial implications, he nevertheless agreed to support me just has he had when we set up the nursery.

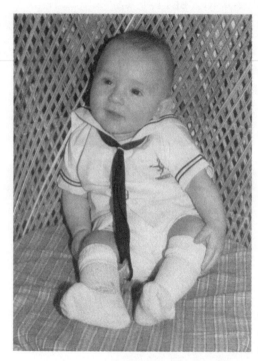

Dan (aged about two months)

Dan and me having fun in the park at Sherburn-in-Elmet

Dan on the riverbank (opposite Victoria House)

My Open University degree ceremony with Alf and Dan (aged three) at Leeds Town Hall

Dan's first day at school

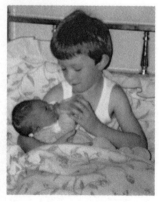

*Dan feeding his
baby sister*

Dan helped me bake and decorate this cake for Nicki's first birthday

Alf with Dan and Nicki at Robin Hood's Bay

Dan and Nicki

Dan, Alf and Nicki in Benodet, Brittany – August 1993 (just before the new school opened)

Victoria House – the four storey property we bought in Goole in 1985. The nursery operated on the lower two floors and we lived on the top two floors

Alf's dad, Alf (Senior) building the sandpit for the nursery

On the lower ground floor – the Messy Room

*Another view of the Messy Room. The children's faces have been
deliberately blurred.*

Cutting and sticking in the Messy Room

*The front playroom (also on the lower ground floor)
with a café theme*

The Front Playroom with a road safety theme

The carpeted play area

The outdoor play area

Story time (one of the first floor rooms with river views)

The Rumpus Room (also on the first floor). In August 1993 these facilities were moved to the new double garage to enable this room to be used as the first classroom for The New School

One of the rooms in the Babes 'n' Tots Annexe

CHAPTER 8

The Ball Starts Rolling
December 1992

At the earliest opportunity after returning from London, I talked about the possibility of a small school with the nursery staff and told them about the flyer I'd drafted to send out to the nursery parents. They seemed a little surprised, as we had a really successful nursery business and the idea of opening a non-fee-paying small primary school sounded rather ambitious to them. Nevertheless, the staff humoured me and expressed their interest. I explained that I planned to organise a public meeting before Christmas to discuss these ideas.

I telephoned Kevin Holloway, from the small school workshop, and explained that the weekend we'd attended had given me the inspiration to open a small school in Goole. I asked him if he would like to be the guest speaker at our forthcoming meeting. He agreed and we set the date for two weeks' time, on Tuesday 15th December. I also phoned up Colin Hodgetts and he agreed to attend a subsequent meeting on Friday 5th February if sufficient interest was shown at the first meeting. And so the flyer I had scribbled out on the train was promptly typed up on headed nursery note paper and given to each of the nursery parents.

** STOP PRESS * *

Are you concerned about your child's future?

- Are you worried about the effects on your child of demoralised teachers and oversized classes in state schools today?
- Are you unhappy about the only real alternative offered today (i.e. independent fee-paying schools, usually with a very formal curriculum)?
- Do you long for a small caring school that can cater for your child's individual needs and encourage high educational standards?
- Do you yearn for your child to be in a class with no more than twelve children?
- Would you like to play a far greater role in your child's education by being involved in planning and decision-making at all levels?
- Would you like to see your child's time more valuably spent, and likewise have the option to spend more time with your child if so desired?
- If you work, would you like a school that offered extended care so you don't have to worry about childminders before or after school?

If you said 'yes' to any of the above questions and would like to consider a serious *non-fee-paying* alternative to a state school education, you are invited to attend a ...

SPECIAL MEETING ON TUESDAY 15TH DECEMBER
at 8.00pm
VENUE TO BE DECIDED

This meeting is being supported in its aims by the Human Scale Education movement, a charitable body established to promote human-scale values in education. Kevin Holloway, an education lecturer at Bretton Hall College, Wakefield, will be at the meeting to represent the views of this growing national movement. Colin Hodgetts, the headteacher of the internationally famous The Small School, Hartland, Devon (also the author of *Inventing a School* and... *as if children matter... SCHOOLS FOR TOMORROW*) has agreed to visit in the new year to promote this project, providing enough interest is shown at the initial meeting.

It would be very helpful to us if you would return the attached slip as soon as possible in order that we may ascertain whether or not a larger venue will need to be organised (the final venue will be displayed in the nursery on Thursday 10th December). Thank you.

WITH YOUR HELP THIS VISION COULD BECOME A
REALITY IN GOOLE FROM SEPT 1993

The initial response to the flyer was good, and I felt we needed to meet in a larger space than I could offer in one of the nursery rooms, so my next step was to organise a different venue for the meeting.

We already had a very good relationship with nearby Riverside Special School, as our nursery had been using their pool for swimming lessons, and their main hall for movement lessons on a weekly basis for a number of years. We also used their field for our annual sports day, and their hall for our annual Christmas concert. I duly contacted Graham Pirt, the headteacher, to see if we could book their school hall for the evening. Fortunately, he agreed.

Not only was I strongly motivated to set up a small school, but there was something else I'd been dreaming of for years, and this seemed that it might just be the perfect opportunity. When Dan was about three, we had a visit from my friend Kath and her two children, Ben (eight) and Dominic (five). Kath had been living in Cyprus for a number of years with her husband and two sons. I was so envious when she told me about their typical school day over there. The boys attended school from 8am until 1pm, then spent the afternoons going swimming, visiting places of interest, playing cards, reading, or some other fun activity together. Ever since Kath had told me this, I'd had a longing to spend similar quality time with my own children. So if a new school was starting from scratch, why couldn't it be on that basis? Especially if optional childcare were available after school from 1pm until 5.30pm for those who needed it.

I imagined a typical continental day to be the ideal way to educate children in partnership with parents. I hadn't had my own children only to pass them over to somebody else as soon as they reached statutory school age. Ever since Dan had started school, I missed that special time we used to have every Tuesday and Thursday afternoon. He was always too exhausted at the end of the school day to want to do any of the special things we used to do. At that particular moment in time, I was enjoying the afternoons with Nicki but would have loved to spend more time with Dan too. I felt so strongly about this that if I was successful in getting the new school off the ground, I would like it to be based on a typical continental day. I believed that a shorter school day with fewer break times would enable parents to spend more time with their children if they so wished, and I didn't think their education would suffer at all; if anything it would be beneficial. My thoughts were really quite radical, as I was not aware of any state schools, or indeed any school, in this country offering a continental day at the time. I am aware that some state schools are starting to introduce the idea of a shorter school day with fewer breaks, but this has only begun to happen quite recently.

And so, at the public meeting, I was going to suggest to parents that the day start at 8.00am and finished at 1.00pm There would be a half-hour break for a substantial mid-morning snack, but otherwise no set breaks. This would give a similar number of teaching hours to a traditional school day. For parents who might have a problem with childcare in the afternoon, we could offer optional afternoon activities at the school. We were also hoping to offer before- and after-school care, as we had already been doing at the nursery for a number of years.

For quite some time, I had believed that a typical continental school day would mean that a child could spend the same amount of time in 'statutory' education, yet more time with his or her own family by merely reducing the break times. I also had other reasons for wanting to reduce break times ...

I was aware that Dan had had some very negative experiences at playtime. He didn't enjoy rough-and-tumble games, and he didn't like playing football, as the other boys did. He spent most playtimes standing at the edge of the playground watching the game from the side. This also led to him being taunted and teased. Just thinking about this brings back painful memories from my own school days. I can recall a time when I was about seven, being painfully shy and having a constant dread of break times. I remember having one-and-a-half-hour lunch breaks, being freezing cold and lonely. It was all right when my best friend, Gaynor, was around, but she had health problems and was frequently absent from school. I can recall the sense of panic I used to feel when she wasn't in class when the register was called, and then dreading the morning playtime bell going. Not only did the bell often signify that I had to stop doing something I was engrossed in, but on the days when Gaynor wasn't there every minute of 'playtime' seemed an eternity. I was far too shy to ask other children if I could join in their games, meaning a long, long break with only my own thoughts for company, often spent wandering around an expansive concrete jungle desperate for the time to pass.

While working as a teacher in traditional schools I have witnessed some children suffering a similar fate to my own and Dan's during playtimes, and whenever possible I used to intervene to help them find a friend or encourage them to join in with a game. For some children, you were aware that playtime was nearly always an ordeal, whether due to shyness, bullying, getting into disputes, or some other reason.

Bringing my thoughts back to the public meeting, having organised the venue my next step was to plan my presentation carefully in order to support my arguments for setting up a small school in Goole with a philosophy modelled on The Small School, Hartland. Of course, their school was for secondary-aged children and ours would be for primary-aged children (initially at least). Their school was based on typical school hours and terms whereas ours would be based on the continental school day with optional activities in the afternoon. We would also offer after-school care from 3.30pm, in addition to school holiday care. So the school would be open from 8am until 5.30pm every day including school holidays (closing for just one week at Christmas). The children attending the school would be expected to attend for the core curriculum times of 8am until 1.00pm throughout school term time but would have the option of additional care and/or attending additional activities at other times.

To support my presentation, I obtained advice on how to use an overhead projector (which I'd never used before), and carefully prepared my main notes using the necessary acetates. Kevin would be covering the background to the philosophy of Human Scale Education, and my task would be to convey my feelings and reasons for preferring the continental school day, and how our plans to open a small school might progress. I prepared some hand-outs showing different options for the school day, with arguments to support the continental or flexi-day and arguments against the typical traditional school day.

MODEL 1: CONTINENTAL SCHOOL DAY

All children to attend 8:00am – 1.00pm (possibly 8.30am – 1.30pm)
During this time the children will follow a carefully planned educational curriculum including English, Maths, Science, Technology, Humanities, PE, Music, Art, French, Personal/Social Education. They will have a substantial snack mid to late morning. There will be no set playtimes as such although the children will use the outdoor facilities as part of their education / social curriculum with the teacher. Children may then be collected at 1.15pm or may stay for a meal followed by optional afternoon activities with care provided up to 5.30pm if required.

Lunch / Optional Activities 1.00pm – 5.30pm (or earlier)
Afternoon activities may include – games; art and crafts; computers; chess; projects; facilities for private study; horse-riding; swimming; French Club; music; dance; use of local leisure centre facilities; environmental group; etc.

MODEL 2: FLEXI-DAY

8.00am – 9.00am – early morning care provided if required

9am – 12 noon – all children to attend core curriculum activities
During this time the children will receive an education based on the carefully planned core curriculum covering most of the aforementioned subjects in a more limited way. There will be a light snack mid-morning and no set playtimes as such although educational / social outdoor activities would be encouraged. As the set educational day is minimal each child would need to follow an additional educational programme… this could be an agreed programme of parent working with the child during the afternoons, or the child attending curriculum enhancement sessions at Victoria House (or elsewhere), or an agreed combination of both to make up basic educational entitlement.

Lunchtime 12.00pm – 1.00pm (playtime will be optional rather than 'enforced')

Optional Curriculum Enhancement – 1.00pm – 4.00pm
Similar to the aforementioned afternoon activities but will possibly include other educational activities required to make up a child's 'full-time' education.

4.00pm – 5.30pm – childcare available if required.

ADVANTAGES OVER TRADITIONAL
SCHOOLING – MODELS 1 & 2

1. Most children are much more alert in the morning.
2. The teacher is more likely to stay enthusiastic for this period of time, having a positive knock-on effect for the children.
3. By having an 'apparently' shorter day the children are more likely to relish the enjoyable time they spend with the teacher.
4. The teacher is more likely to return refreshed the next day after an afternoon spent with his/her own family or pursuing some other outside interest (again, obviously better for the children).
5. The children will not pick up the negative 'vibes' of bullying and boredom of traditional school playtimes.
6. The teacher will have more time to plan and record – also to undertake further training – again, a very positive outcome for the children.
7. Parents will be able to enjoy more of their children if that is what they want – even if only for the precious afternoon outing when they have an occasional day off work – a privilege usually denied them in a state school.
8. Parents may make use of the opportunity either to be involved in the education of their child at home, or become involved with other parents/helpers in the running of the afternoon sessions.

9.   Parents who need to work can rest assured that their children will be enjoying the afternoon sessions and don't have to worry about finding alternative care before or after school.

10. Model 1 will only require a teacher for 0.8 of the usual teaching time, and Model 2, 0.6 teaching time – thus reducing the cost of employing a teacher. Parents and/or other helpers could be trained to run the afternoon sessions, probably under the guidance of a qualified leader.

11. In many state primary schools most of the 'formal' education takes place during the mornings anyway – so in this respect the ideas are not so radical.

12. As models 1 & 2 are quite unique in their entire format we are more likely to remain high profile – this would make it easier to receive funding and sponsorship from commercial organisations.

NB: All parents will be expected to raise or contribute 25% of the costs involved in offering the basic curriculum. In addition, parents requiring the afternoon sessions will be expected to raise or contribute an agreed amount towards the cost of these sessions or offer services in lieu. We will endeavour to receive additional charitable funding for the afternoon sessions if at all possible.

MODELS 3 – EXAMPLE OF TYPICAL TRADITIONAL SCHOOL DAY

9.00am – 10.15am	National Curriculum Work
10.15am – 10.30am	Playtime (Teacher on playground duty)
10.30am – 12.15pm	Resume work
12.15pm – 1.15pm	Lunch & playtime (lunchtime supervisors on duty)
1.15pm – 2.15pm	Learning through play / arts & crafts
2.15pm – 2.30pm	Playtime (Teacher on playground duty)
2.30pm – 3.30pm	Learning through play / music / stories

DISADVANTAGES OF TYPICAL DAY

1. Generally no care available before and after school.
2. Often time is lost before each playtime when children stop and tidy up (sometimes when they are enthralled in an activity or just beginning to grasp a new concept) and change into outdoor clothing.
3. Likewise valuable time is lost getting children changed again after each playtime and it can take some time for children to settle down again.
4. Children may have to go out in cold weather in inadequate clothing.
5. Children may get bullied at playtime – or even become a bully!
6. Children may suffer boredom – may wish they could be inside finishing off their work (often not allowed) or be doing something more stimulating.
7. Emotional / social pressures of playground jungle – most children have no preparation in how to cope with such pressures. Staffing levels at playtime are often inadequate (usually no specialised training is given on outdoor play).
8. Most schools are ill equipped for constructive playground learning to take place – most schools have no specialised play equipment. Can you imagine taking your child to a bare expanse of concrete three times a day and finding enough to do?
9. To survive in the playground jungle a child may have to learn some rather cruel peer group rules, and will undoubtedly pick up the specialised playground language!
10. Apart from the annual two weeks' holiday entitlement, parents are unable to take children out of school if they so wish to spend extra time with them at home – even if the parent intends to offer some individual home teaching.

A few days before the inaugural meeting was due to take place, I thought that press coverage might be useful in helping to increase awareness of the school, promote the number of pupils, and perhaps help to attract funding from charitable trusts; so I dropped a poster off at each of the two local newspapers based in Goole. I also informed a contact at the *Yorkshire Post*. This resulted in the latter sending one of their photographers to the nursery on the day the meeting was to be held, and their reporter Anita Brown phoning me for some more information.

Alf shared some of the growing excitement leading up to the public meeting as I went through my presentation with him. In addition to presenting the basic proposal and explaining how the school was going to work and the philosophy behind the project, I had already prepared a list of pros and cons in anticipation of some of the questions I'd be asked. I became increasingly nervous as the day approached.

On the day of the meeting Kevin Holloway travelled from his workplace at Bretton Hall College, Wakefield (approximately forty miles away), to our home above the nursery in Goole, where he met Alf, Dan and Nicki for the first time. Sitting around our pine kitchen table, we enjoyed a meal of stuffed courgettes and couscous, followed by a fresh fruit salad. Kevin said he loved the gothic arched windows and the view of the river with the fields beyond. He expressed an interest in the river traffic, about which Dan enlightened him, explaining that cargo boats going in one direction were heading for York, whereas if they were going in the opposite direction they would usually be heading out towards the Humber and perhaps the sea beyond. I passed the comment that Dan and Nicki had seen many more boats going past our house than they ever had double-decker buses. Alf mentioned that on a clear day we could see Scunthorpe across the fields. Nicki asked Kevin if he had any children, and Kevin told her that he had a son called Matthew, who was slightly older than Dan, and a daughter, Laura, who was slightly older than Nicki. Numerous questions followed from the children, which poor Kevin answered as best he could. It wasn't long before Dan expressed a desire to meet Matthew as they shared some common interests, and likewise Nicki expressed a desire to meet Laura.

After the meal and lively conversation, Alf supervised Dan and Nicki getting ready for bed in preparation for the babysitter's arrival, while I went through my presentation notes with Kevin. All seemed well: the babysitter arrived, we kissed the children goodnight, and set off to Riverside School with great anticipation of what might come to be.

Shortly after Kevin, Alf and I arrived at the school, several nursery staff started to arrive to help set out chairs, prepare refreshments, and set up an information display. Kevin helped me set up the projector and screen.

Ten minutes before the meeting was due to start Lynn Steggles, a senior reporter from the local paper the *Times and Chronicle*, arrived. He was followed within moments by Kassie Holliday, editor of the *Goole Courier*. They both said hello to me as they entered, and I introduced them to Kevin. The nursery staff handed them a selection of leaflets and hand-outs from the information stall, and they then sat down together on the front row, seemingly discussing the contents of the leaflets. Parents of children at my nursery started to arrive. Initially I greeted them individually and introduced each of them to Kevin, but that became more difficult as more people came in. So the parents who arrived later just received a nod and a smile from me. There were also one or two parents I didn't recognise, who must have heard about the meeting on the grapevine. I was becoming increasingly nervous as I sat at the front of the hall with Kevin, and found myself taking deep breaths. I counted over thirty people sitting in the audience.

One more deep breath, and I stood up and welcomed everybody. I started by explaining why I felt there was a need for a new school in Goole. I then formally introduced Kevin, explaining how we had recently met at the Human Scale Education training event in London.

Kevin began to speak about his role as Head of Maths Education at Bretton Hall Teacher Training College. He talked about his observations of teachers and children in state schools, and how some children's needs were not being met due to class size and restrictions of the National Curriculum. Sometimes, he said, it seemed that because of the prescriptive nature of the National Curriculum and the demands of assessment and testing, children were like items on a conveyor belt. The philosophy of Human Scale Education was explained, especially the emphasis on the relationships within the school between teachers, pupils and parents. He went on to explain some of the things we learned at our training event in London.

It was then my turn to speak again. Taking another deep breath, I expanded upon my vision of why the school should be non-fee-paying, how we could set it up, the role of parents, and my belief in the advantages of a continental day. The concept of the continental school day was an alien one to many of the parents, but they listened to my arguments and many seemed to understand my reasoning behind the idea. The main concern for most of the parents was that we were offering a 'free' core curriculum from 8am to 1pm: parents who worked said they would be out of pocket if they had to pay additional childcare between school ending at 1pm or 1.30pm and the usual school finish time of 3.30pm

Many parents had concerns about the financial implications and where the new school would be situated. I said that, if necessary, it was quite possible to change the use of the rooms on the upper ground floor of the nursery to accommodate up to twenty-five children of primary-school age. The upper ground floor consisted of two large bay-windowed rooms, a cloakroom with a toilet and sink with large storage cupboards, and a good-sized hallway. One of the rooms was currently being used as a Rumpus Room (climbing frame, slide and soft play equipment); the other was divided into two sections, half of it being a Quiet Room with a large table that eight children could comfortably sit around, and two computers set up by the wall, and the other half (beyond a dividing screen) currently being used as a Staff/Parent Area with a range of easy chairs. This room also contained large purpose-built store-cupboards that not only accommodated a range of equipment including books, a range of fabrics, reams of A4 and A3 paper, art paper and rolls of frieze paper, but also had specially designed narrow shelves for different colours of very large sheets of paper (A1 size). All very useful for storing the vast range of paper and other resources we would need for the new school. We had just finished building a double garage to the rear of the playground with the intention of using it for our own cars, but as it had not yet been used, it would be possible to paint the interior and put heating in so that the Rumpus Room facilities could be moved there. This would free up at least one of the large Victorian rooms to be used as a classroom for primary-aged children.

Questions were also being asked about what would happen to the children when they reached secondary-school age. I started to explain about Dame Catherine Harpur's School in Ticknall, Derbyshire. This was a former village primary school which the local county council had planned to close. Concerned villagers contacted Human Scale Education asking for help to prevent the school's closure. At that time Philip Toogood was the coordinator of HSE and he recommended that the history of the school building be explored. It was discovered that the school did not belong to the county council at all, but was held in a trust founded by Dame Catherine Harpur in 1744. The trust deed stated that the building belonged to the villages of Calke and Ticknall for the purposes of providing free education. Following on from this discovery, the community asked Philip Toogood and his wife Annabel to become the first teachers at the school, which they did in 1987. After a few years Philip felt that the older primary children would benefit from being allowed to stay at the school when they reached secondary-school age, and he subsequently allowed the school to grow organically in this way.

Overall, the majority of parents in the audience expressed great interest in the project and could see the potential of a new small school. Others were interested but had serious concerns about financial and practical implications. It was unanimously agreed, however, that possibilities for opening a small school in

Goole should be explored further through a series of meetings. Two meeting dates were set for after Christmas: Thursday 7th January for people who wanted to be on the steering group, and Thursday 14th January for parents interested in sending their children to the school. Both meetings were arranged to take place in the nursery.

CHAPTER 9

Media Attention
(December 1992–September 1993)

The day after the public meeting, the respected regional newspaper the *Yorkshire Post* published a substantial piece entitled '*Funding sought for alternative school*', with the sub-heading, '*Nursery owner plans flexible primary education*'. The article accurately portrayed the reasoning behind the setting up of the small school, referring to the intended continental day, the financial backing needed, and the fact that it would be based on the philosophy of Human Scale Education. The article also mentioned that if successful as a primary school, a small secondary school may also be set up along similar lines a year or two later. A really nice photo of five of the nursery children and myself in the nursery garden accompanied the piece.

The following day, on 17th December 1992, the story made the front page of both the Goole-based newspapers. Unfortunately, though, both the reporters who had attended the meeting had picked up on Kevin's reference to state schools being like 'conveyor belts' and used this terminology in their opening paragraphs. This made me feel somewhat uneasy. Kevin had made this reference when talking about the principles of Human Scale Education, saying that schools should be more like families than factories, and that this was how he regarded the system when he observed his students. What he had actually said was, *'Sometimes it seems that because of the prescriptive nature of the National Curriculum and the demands of the assessment and testing, children are like items on a conveyor belt.'* It just goes to show how the press works, though, doesn't it? I could see that, from the way the statement was depicted in each article, the teachers at the local schools with whom I had worked so closely in the past might regard me as something of a traitor, since it came across as something I had personally said.

During the public meeting I had been especially careful not to say anything negative or detrimental about the local schools because I had worked towards building good relationships with them for years. In the past, local headteachers had recommended my nursery to parents; staff from local schools had attended my open days and training events; and some schools had even sent their staff to my nursery for a full day to gain work experience. I had always been welcomed by local schools when I met them to discuss children who were transferring from the nursery to their school. From this moment on, however, I feared that my good relationship with local schools had been badly tarnished, if not destroyed forever.

Apart from the reference to the 'conveyor belt', and a rather unflattering photo of me, the *Goole Times and Chronicle* produced a really good article. The paper's headlines were, ***'Bold plan for new school',*** with the sub-heading, *'A unique primary school run entirely by parents could be operating in Goole by next*

September'. It continued: *'More than thirty parents gathered together at Riverside School on Tuesday evening to hear nursery school principal Rosalyn Spencer describe her dream of a primary school where there was one teacher to every eight pupils, where each child could learn at its own pace and where there was always time to talk … her vision is of a place where the welfare and development of the child are paramount, not only in academic learning but in personal and social growth too …'*

The other local paper, the *Goole Courier*, carried the headline: ***'Goole to get new style school?'*** It stated: *'Goole is poised for the establishment of an "alternative school" with the aim of avoiding the "conveyor belt" style of education offered by state schools …'* Unfortunately the whole tone of this article focused on negativity towards the state education system rather than the element of choice and individualised learning the new school would promote. I felt that this was another nail in the coffin of my relationship with local schools.

Two days later, on 19th December, the *Yorkshire Evening Press*, which covered the areas of York (twenty-three miles away) and Selby (just thirteen miles from Goole) had an article headed, ***'School to open for business next year'.*** Although there was no reference to the 'conveyor belt' in this article, it did state: *'It's an idea pioneered by Human Scale Education Movement which says that schools should be more like families than factories and that parents should be more involved in what their children study'*. It went on to quote me as saying, *'I don't want to knock state schools, which work very hard, but they operate under difficult conditions with huge numbers of pupils. The parents, including some from Selby, have been asking about a project like this for years to extend* *the caring environment we have here in the nursery into the children's later education. We still need to put a lot of hard work into this plan because we're at a very early stage, but if everything goes smoothly then perhaps we could aim at taking the first children in next September.'*

On 18th January 1993, the *Hull Daily Mail* published a full-page feature about the prospective new school. Under the bold heading, '*In a class of their own?'*

Bob Kernohan, the paper's education reporter, opened the article with, '*A classroom where teaching is based around the individual education, spiritual and emotional needs of each child is the dream of one North Humberside mum. For some local parents, her system based on the Human Scale Education movement is the ideal answer to opting out of state schools. They are backing her scheme to open a pioneering primary which could become a model for schools across the country.'* The first part of the article described the philosophy and principles behind the project. Another part involved feedback from parents who had been interviewed by the reporter. Accountant John Drew is quoted as saying: '*I had never heard of HSE until Rosalyn Spencer drew our attention to it. But it appeals to us because it provides education in an environment controlled in terms of numbers and involves parental input. It is early days yet and we do not know if the project can be funded. But it does offer the chance of a better education for children of parents who cannot afford or do not want to send their children to traditional private schools.'* Another parent, Graeme Matravers, comments on the benefits of an education tailored to meet the individual needs of the child, rather than the child having to fit into the existing system. He said: '*Examinations should not be the be all and end all of education. The teacher–children ratio at this school could only be matched by private fee-paying schools. I believe it will provide a much happier environment.*'

Eager to present a balanced point of view, the *Hull Daily Mail* feature also printed an interview with Humberside's education chief on the local County Council, who urged parents to think very carefully before getting involved in the project. He talks about many pitfalls and the fact that the children may have nobody of their own age group to socialise with. He said he had a colleague in Devon who was aware of The Small School in Hartland, and with regard to this the councillor says: '*They get volunteers including retired teachers to go in and give specialist lessons, but it has to be a nonsense because they lack the facilities and resources of our state schools.*' He continued by saying that he hoped the small school proposal would not go ahead, and that if it did the county might have a legal duty to check it out to make sure the children were receiving a proper education!

My thoughts in response to the councillor's comments were that it is good for children to mix socially with children of different ages, and that this is something that happens naturally within families anyway. Most adults have friends of different ages, and in most areas of employment different ages work together. To me, it is unnatural to put thirty children of the same year group in a class together: it creates artificial barriers between age groups within a school, and it is unlikely that thirty children of the same age have reached the same stage of physical development, and/or the same level of maturity, not to mention intellectual ability. Having children of the same age grouped together causes a number of social problems such as peer group pressure, sometimes unhealthy competition and/or bullying, and can lead to children who do not fit the perceived norm experiencing insurmountable problems that can be seriously detrimental to their emotional well-being. Just because we've had many years of classes of thirty children or more all of the same age, doesn't mean it's right.

With regard to the negative comment the councillor made about volunteers and retired teachers, and a lack of facilities and resources, I would argue firstly that although facilities and resources are important to some extent, the quality of teaching and the quality of the relationships within the school are far more important. Volunteers and retired teachers wanting to impart their knowledge enthusiastically for 'love' rather than as a duty must surely be an asset to any school (providing, of course, adequate supervision is in place). The majority of adults, if you ask them what they were good at at school, can remember doing well in a subject in which they had a teacher who they liked and respected. I don't usually hear adults saying that the facilities and resources had a profound effect on them.

Regarding the final comment about checks on educational standards, the school would be registered with the Department for Education, and Her Majesty's Inspectors would take care of this concern.

A week or so later, I was contacted by BBC Radio Humberside and was asked to give my first ever radio interview. A reporter came to my home, and over a cup of coffee in the kitchen he chatted informally to me about the project before producing an enormous microphone and asking me to carry on chatting just as we had been doing. Easier said than done, as my mouth completely dried up and my mind went partially blank on production of the microphone; but nevertheless the deed was done and the interview went out on the local radio station the following day.

And so it went on and on. We started getting regular coverage in the two Goole-based papers and were also getting coverage in the *Hull Daily Mail*, the *Yorkshire Post*, the *Yorkshire Evening Press* and interviews on BBC Radio Humberside.

Meanwhile, as the local media coverage continued, a storm was brewing. On 4th March 1993, a local headteacher had a long letter published in the local paper. She was referring to all the media coverage of the alternative small school being set up in the town. She strongly defended the current education system and argued the strengths of the National Curriculum. I felt compelled to respond in defence of what I was trying to achieve.

My lengthy letter of response was published in the following week's edition of the paper. Amongst other points, I argued that: *'No two children have exactly the same needs, no two families have exactly the same beliefs. Whereas state schools can meet the needs of many children, they cannot meet them all. Indeed The New School, Goole, is only intended to meet the needs of a small group of children. Other groups will have very different needs and could perhaps consider setting up their own school! What I am talking about now is a system that has been working successfully in Denmark since the 1930s, that is, parents setting up a school with state funding. Ten per cent of schools in Denmark are run by parents and receive 85% government funding. In Holland parent-run schools receive 100% government funding.'* I also gave the reasoning behind the school's proposed continental day, and mentioned the problems some children encountered during long lunch breaks with a very high ratio of children to each lunchtime supervisor. I was totally unaware at that time how badly my comments could be taken out of context.

The following week the local paper printed a very long and very angry letter from the chair of governors of the primary school whose headteacher had written the first letter. The letter not only slammed me and my ideas personally, it took almost everything I had written out of context. The chair of governors argued that the lunchtime supervisors in her school were all highly trained and highly respected individuals (I never implied that they weren't, I was referring to the adult:child ratio). She went on to say that bullying never took place in her school, due a range of lunchtime activities.

The published letter was very personal and very hurtful. I thought about ways in which I could respond in an effort to correct her misconceptions. But then I had no wish to be spiteful or petty and did not wish to see this matter escalate out of all proportion. So rather than responding in the paper, which I was sorely tempted to do to save face if nothing else, I decided instead to phone the headteacher who had been responsible for the original letter in an attempt to bury the hatchet. We had a long chat during which she let it be known that the very first newspaper articles referring to state schools being like factory conveyor belts had really upset the apple-cart locally, with headteachers phoning each other in anger and disbelief. I explained to her that the papers gave the impression that those particular words were mine, when in fact they were not, and explained that what the new school wanted to offer was a choice, especially for children who found mainstream education difficult. That some children could just not cope with the inflexibility and impersonal nature of the current system was a fact that could not be denied, and some children would only be able to thrive in small, more personal setting. Although the headteacher and I differed on our educational philosophy, we agreed that it was best to let matters lie now. I agreed that I would not write to the letters' page again regarding the incident, and she agreed to do likewise.

The following edition of the weekly paper, however, contained something I had known nothing about beforehand. Somebody else had written in on the subject. The author of the signed letter explained that he was an ex-teacher who after many years had given up teaching because he had become so unhappy with the current state education system. His letter said that he had been watching the development of the small school with interest and he agreed with the arguments put forward to set up such a school. He said that he knew of a great number of ex-teachers who had left the profession through disillusionment. As for the chair of governors who had had her letter published in the previous week's paper, she would have to have been incredibly thick-skinned to cope with the detrimental comments now aimed personally at her. The writer said that *anyone who could say that bullying does not occur in their school is too naïve and ignorant to be chair of governors*. He suggested that perhaps this was the only school in the country where everything was as rosy as she had depicted in her letter. I had been hurt by her response to my letter, but now I felt incredibly sorry for the woman – I'm sure she must have wished that the floor could open up and swallow her.

The local newspaper coverage continued with regular updates on the prospect of a new alternative-style school opening in Goole. Some of the articles were accurate and helpful in promoting the opening of the small school. Some articles were not so accurate, but I was beginning to get used to that now.

Looking back, I should have had reservations about media coverage, but in reality I'm not sure if it could have been prevented even if I hadn't contacted the papers first. On the positive side the coverage made some people think about possible alternatives to mainstream education. It also helped attract support for the school, whether prospective pupils or help being offered by educationalists sympathetic with the philosophy of the school. On the other hand, it caused a lot of harm by damaging the relationships I had built up with schools in the years I'd been running my nursery. Then again, I suppose by the very nature of what I was trying to do I was questioning the system, and that alone would have made local teachers feel defensive.

CHAPTER 10

Gathering Momentum
(December 1992–February 1993)

After that first meeting on 15th December, I knew I'd set the wheels in motion for a momentous change, not only in my own life, but others' too. Up until that moment, I'd been getting on with my life relatively quietly in a respectable fashion as a mum and nursery owner; now I knew there was no going back. The media were involved and I felt exposed. I wasn't really sure that I wanted to draw attention to myself in this way; all I'd wanted initially was something better for Dan. Now I felt that there were a considerable number of people looking at me with disapproval after my – seemingly bizarre – act of trying to create something that, at that moment in time, seemed like an impossible dream. Who was I to be criticising mainstream education in this way? It was while I was feeling a little raw and wobbly like this, after making front page news with the 'conveyor belt' implications, that I received an unexpected visitor at the nursery …

I immediately recognised the tall, bespectacled man with the kind face and smiling eyes as Mike Smith, a well-known and highly regarded local figure. I'd never met him personally, but I knew quite a few things about him. He had played a key role in the production of the Howden Town Play, a massive undertaking in the neighbouring town of Howden. The play had involved over a hundred local people from the town and surrounding area, and had been a resounding success. I'd been to see the play with Alf, and regarded it as an amazing, innovative, production. I was also aware that Mike was a teacher, head of English at a large secondary school in Howden.

Mike told me that he had read the newspaper coverage with great interest and was excited at the possibility of such a school being set up in Goole. He said he'd come along to visit me to see if there was anything he could do to help. As I welcomed Mike in, I couldn't help feeling extremely flattered that he'd taken the trouble to come and visit me. I invited him upstairs to our private living quarters so that we could talk more easily, and offered him a cup of tea. Mike said he had heard of Human Scale Education and wholeheartedly supported its philosophy. We chatted for some time about the project and how it had come about. Mike admitted he was unhappy about teaching within the constraints of mainstream education and was looking forward to a time, in the not too distant future, when he could resign from teaching in the state system and set up his own business. He expanded on this, saying he would like to offer English to schools in a more exciting way, through drama, poetry and writing. Before he left, Mike offered to be an unpaid adviser for our English curriculum, and agreed to leading an evening for prospective parents looking at effective ways of teaching English, and how parents could help their children.

I don't know if Mike was ever aware of the impact his visit

had on me, but after he had left I was filled with a sense of assurance that I was definitely doing the right thing. I knew it wasn't going to be easy, yet having Mike believe so sincerely in what I was trying to achieve, and his offer of help, gave me a vast amount of inner strength.

Mike wasn't the only one to offer support. Lynn Steggles, the senior reporter for the *Times and Chronicle*, expressed a particular interest in what the school was trying to achieve. He told me he had been a deputy head with over thirty years' teaching experience, and that he supported our aims and objectives. He too offered his services as a volunteer curriculum adviser for the new school.

Christmas came and went. It was already Thursday 7th January, the date of our first steering-group meeting. There was a feeling of anticipation and excitement as we met together in one of the nursery rooms. The very pleasing turnout included senior reporter Lynn Steggles; Kevin Holloway (who travelled from Wakefield again); and Colin Luckett, a local solicitor I had got to know through the local Greenpeace group. Getting down to business, we needed to appoint a group of trustees to look at drawing up a constitution and applying for charitable status. Colin said he'd be happy to take the lead on this. We looked at the Department for Education requirements for room sizes and facilities in order to register for independent school status. We were fortunate to have three local accountants who agreed to work together to look at costings. We decided to set up a separate group for fund-raising, since raising 75% of the running costs as The Small School in Hartland had, would take a tremendous amount of organising.

A week later, on Thursday 14th January, parents who were

interested in sending their children to the school attended a meeting at the nursery. This gathering was also well attended. Following on from the first public meeting in December, the subject of the 'continental day' was discussed. The parents felt that 8am was too early to start the day, so it was agreed that the core curriculum would be from 8.30am until 1.30pm, although the school would still be open from 8am for those who wished to attend earlier. It was also agreed that the optional activities from 1.30pm until 3.30pm would be part of the 'free' package, but that care after 3.30pm would need to be paid for. The majority of parents were happy with this arrangement.

In the group was a parent who was also a local accountant. He expressed concern about offering 'free' education. He said he had been interested in his three children attending the new school, but he argued that fees were essential if the school were to survive. He didn't want his children to start at a school only for it to close down due to lack of funding. He was uncertain as to whether or not the school would be able to obtain the 75% trust funding we would need to operate effectively. I argued that to charge fees would be to go against the HSE principles that education should be free to all. It was hoped that if a number of small schools similar to The Small School at Hartland were set up, as we were planning to do and as was beginning to happen elsewhere as a result of the HSE's work in this direction, the government would start to offer subsidies based on models in Denmark and Holland. Everybody else in the group was against the charging of fees but agreed that 'voluntary' contributions would need to be made in one way or another, whether of money or time.

One of the parents, Christina, said that she was happy to take the lead on fund-raising, and would also start writing to charitable trusts for funding once we had our constitution in place. I explained that Human Scale Education was happy for us to be officially affiliated, and to refer to their charitable status. This would mean that we could start applying for funding prior to our own charitable status being finalised, as that could take some time. Christina said that, in that case, she'd get started straightaway.

The parents' meeting ended with a debate about what the school should be called. After a lively discussion with a few different names being proposed, it was eventually decided that it should simply be called The New School.

A week later trustees were officially appointed, with Colin being elected as chairperson at the first meeting. Despite having to travel so far, Kevin Holloway remained a dedicated supporter and became a key member of the group. Jean Kitchen (an active member of the local Liberal Democrats, later to become a councillor, then Goole's town mayor), was not only a good friend of mine and Alf's but was also very interested in education, and she also agreed to become a trustee. Other trustees included a local businessman, an accountant, and an organic farmer. The trustees got to work immediately on seeking charitable status.

February was fast approaching, and I was looking forward to our next big event for which posters and flyers had been distributed around Goole. In large lettering, heading the poster, were the words:

... *as if children matter*
SCHOOLS FOR TOMORROW

with a picture of three children playing football together. This was followed by lettering of appropriate sizes to ensure the required impact:

A talk given by
COLIN HODGETTS

Headteacher of The Small School, Hartland, and recently returned from a speaking tour of Japan and India.

Colin Hodgetts will talk about the philosophy and the practicalities involved in the founding of a small school based on human scale values

(Donation to HSE costs at the door)

The poster ended with the address of the larger venue of Riverside School, an HSE logo, and The Small School's logo of a hand holding a lighted candle.

On the afternoon of 5th February 1993, I drove to Leeds train station (an eighty-mile round trip) to collect Colin and two pupils who attended his school, in preparation for the talk at Riverside that evening. I greeted Colin as he came through the platform gates, and was introduced to Olivia (fifteen) and Lisa (thirteen). On the journey from the station to Goole, Olivia and Lisa expressed their interest in the industrial landscape they were passing through, which looked very different to Devon. As we travelled by car along the M62 the girls asked about the tall chimney stacks and cooling towers of three power stations, namely, Ferrybridge, Eggborough and then Drax (the largest coal-fired power station in Europe). Their questions led on to a discussion about the mining communities, and the political aspects of recent mine closures. I was quite relieved that Colin confidently answered their questions in much more depth than I could have done.

Arriving safely at our home above the nursery, I showed Colin and the two girls where they would be sleeping that night and gave them chance to relax before the meal. Kevin Holloway arrived from work in time to join us for some cauliflower moussaka before we set off to Riverside School.

As the meeting had been widely promoted in newspaper articles as well as the posters I'd distributed around town, it was very well attended. Colin spoke about The Small School in Hartland and then Olivia and Lisa spoke very confidently about their experiences there. There was an interesting question and answer session involving the audience and our three guest speakers. Olivia and Lisa answered their questions very impressively. The audience then turned to Colin to ask questions about the financial viability of the proposed school. This was the main area of concern. Some parents still thought fees should be charged in an effort to overcome their anxieties. They said that they would definitely register their children if it was agreed to charge fees, and wouldn't be sending them if we continued to go down the trust fund and voluntary contributions route. Colin again confirmed the HSE philosophy that free education should be available to all. I also remained determined that the school should run on voluntary contributions from parents with the aim of achieving charitable funding. I just hoped that our school would be as successful operating in this way as The Small School in Hartland had been.

The following morning Colin was due to give a live three-minute interview for BBC Radio Humberside. We left Olivia and Lisa having breakfast with Alf, Dan and Nicki while Colin and I set off on the ten minute walk into town where there was a tiny recording studio. We'd been given instructions for the collection of the key to the studio. Once inside, Colin seemed to know what he had to do to set himself up with the headphones. You could tell he'd done this a few times before. After an initial phone call to say we had arrived and were already set up, the interview began. I was more nervous about it than Colin was, and I wasn't even speaking! Colin was asked some very challenging questions about The Small School and his thoughts on the proposed new school, all of which he dealt with in a calm and confident way. The radio presenter seemed to be duly impressed by Colin's arguments in support of The New School in Goole and extended his live air time to ten minutes.

After the interview, Colin and I took the more leisurely walk back to the house along the riverbank. Colin wanted to know more about the River Ouse, the types of boats that travelled past our house, and Goole Docks. I can also recall a lively discussion about environmental issues.

Back at the house there was just time to make Colin, Olivia and Lisa a pack-up for their long journey home before they set off back along the M62 to catch their train.

Following the public meetings and the subsequent publicity, a growing number of people had become involved in The New School project. These could be divided into five main groups. First, the parents who were interested in their children attending the school; secondly, the children who were likely to be our first intake of pupils; thirdly, educationalists offering their professional expertise; fourthly, local professionals willing to become trustees of the project; and finally, the steering group, who were going to carry out and manage a substantial number of tasks before the school could open. Lots of peripheral decisions still had to be made, and we were still considering alternative premises, staffing, and the massive question of funding ...

CHAPTER 11

Getting to Know
Each Other
(March 1993–September 1993)

At one of the earlier parents' meetings, it was agreed that we would run a series of evening workshops for any parents interested in getting involved in The New School.

We started off one evening by having a Maths Workshop led by Kevin Holloway. He talked to the parents about his love of maths, and how, if taught well, maths could be an exciting and fun subject. An enjoyable time was had by all experimenting with mathematical equipment and completing the puzzles he'd brought along.

I also took advantage of Mike Smith's offer of help, and he was delighted to lead an English Workshop for parents. I can recall a very useful exercise where he showed us a set of pictures and then put some symbols we didn't recognise underneath each picture. He asked us if we could work out which letter each symbol represented so that we could read the story. Some adults were confident that they could crack the code; some felt inadequate because they couldn't see a pattern. In the end even the confident adults were not quite sure they were going to solve it. That was when Mike explained, with a knowing smile on his face, that the symbols didn't represent anything. He asked us how we all felt about the activity. The adults there described the different levels of anxiety and embarrassment they had felt at the thought that they might be the only one who couldn't make sense of the symbols. Mike then explained that that was frequently how dyslexic pupils felt in school when confronted with words that looked like a jumble. It was a very good way of helping everybody there to understand how a child with learning difficulties could feel in the classroom, especially when other children could do something they could not.

As plans to open The New School gained momentum, it was also decided that it would be a good idea to set up a Saturday Morning Club so that prospective children could get to know each other. I thought these important steps would lead to a sense of community. Based initially in the nursery, the club met from 10am to 12 noon every Saturday. In addition to a range of activities such as puzzles, games, model-building, and baking, there would usually be an art and craft activity available (with all the activities being adapted accordingly for the different age groups). Playing cooperative games with a parachute became a firm favourite. At the end of each session we usually gathered together for a shared musical activity. Often the children and their parents would join in together.

Sometimes outings were organised for the Saturday Morning Club. A couple of the parents were farmers, and they willingly proposed their farms as a venue. I can clearly recall one cold, rather wet Saturday morning when the children arrived in raincoats, hats and wellies to explore the woods of a farm in South Duffield. During a particularly heavy downpour, everybody had to squash into a small wooden hut in the middle of the woods for shelter. This was a rather comical experience, as all the children were giggling at the sound of the rain hammering down on the roof. Returning to the farmhouse after the rain had eased, the children dried themselves in front of the fire while enjoying hot chocolate and biscuits.

On another occasion, we visited Graeme's organic sheep farm in Babthorpe, near Selby, where on arrival, we were led into a large barn to see some newborn lambs. The children could hardly contain their excitement as Graeme carefully showed each one of them how to feed a lamb with milk from a baby's bottle. Poor Graeme had to deal with an almost endless stream of questions (which I'm pleased to say he dealt with in his usual cheerful, unflappable manner) until he was rescued by his wife arriving in the barn with a large tray of refreshments. There was a place for the children to wash their hands after stroking the sheep and lambs, before each of them found a place to sit on a haystack. They then chattered away to each other, making further observations about the animals while enjoying their drinks and home-made scones.

Sometimes a family played host to the Saturday Morning Club and we'd visit their house to play games in the garden or do an activity around the kitchen table. On one occasion we went to Christina's house and had a Chinese-themed morning. As well as sampling Chinese food and making lanterns, the children learned how to sing the Chinese version of 'Twinkle Twinkle Little Star' while I accompanied them on my guitar. On another occasion the Club met at our caravan in Filey for a full day, enjoying a walk on the beach, freshly made doughnuts, sandcastles, and paddling in the sea.

A strong community spirit was starting to develop amongst all those involved in trying to get The New School off the ground. In addition to the children getting to know each other and getting to know the adults involved in the project, the parents were also starting to form a community. I found this quite exhilarating, and it helped to feed the energy and enthusiasm needed to proceed with such an ambitious project.

Fund-raising was a constant effort, and wherever possible a fund-raising activity (such as a raffle) was brought into social gatherings. On one occasion, in July, I remember a particularly large fund-raising gathering when everybody involved in the project made an effort to attend a barbecue at Graeme's farm. We enjoyed glorious sunshine all day and after we had eaten some delicious food, we enjoyed a game of rounders. I remember this occasion particularly well, as Kevin Holloway joined us for the day with his two children, Matthew and Laura. We talked about plans for the school, and Graeme said that he'd like to be involved in working with the children to teach them some basic principles of organic life. He also suggested a tree-planting day in the autumn.

We held a number of other events. On one occasion a parent organised a fashion show, and another parent set up an auction for which people donated either an item or services (such as babysitting or cooking a meal). I remember that the most popular auction prize (donated by a local business) was a hot-air balloon flight, complete with a bottle of champagne!

All these events took a lot of time and energy to organise and support, and despite all the hours put in, they only raised pounds rather than the thousands we needed. I'd bought some fund-raising directories and Christina took on the daunting task of writing to the organisations listed one by one, appealing for financial support. I also spent time writing to potential trusts whenever I could, but Christina did the bulk of this work.

After many, many hours of writing letters to trust funds, nothing had been raised. And for all the time we'd spent organising fundraising activities, we had only raised a grand total of £1,500. Although it was my ambition that we open as a non-fee-paying school, part of our agreement with parents was that everybody try to make a 'voluntary' contribution of some kind. Those that could afford it had agreed to make a financial contribution (even as little as £5 a month), whereas those who couldn't should agree to give a set amount of time to a specific task each week, such as cleaning, gardening, additional fund-raising, or, under the supervision of a teacher, sharing a skill (such as art and crafts) with the children. Things weren't looking good at all, when one parent came to me saying that she could afford to pay fees for her child to have a place at a local fee-paying independent school and yet had made the choice to send her child to us. She knew that I was opposed to the charging of fees, and that it was against the principles of Human Scale Education, but she insisted on making a donation equivalent to the fees she would have paid had she chosen the traditional independent school option. Her offer was extremely generous and brought the combined total of raised funds and parental donations to around £5,000. I was well aware, however, that that was not nearly enough to set up a school.

Time was running out and decisions needed to be made. What should we do? Should we accept defeat and admit that the project wasn't viable?

I had been hoping that enough money would be raised to pay a teacher to run the school so that I could continue to run the nursery. There didn't seem to be any chance of that happening. The only way I could see for the school to open was for me to volunteer my services as teacher, working initially for no wage. And although ideally The New School would have separate premises to the nursery, the only viable option was to offer the use of a room within the nursery.

Unfortunately for poor Alf, there was only one decision I felt I could make, as we had not put in all this effort to fail. And if the school didn't open, what would happen to Dan? What would happen to Nicki? And what would happen to all the other children who had been coming to the Saturday Morning Club and were looking forward to being part of The New School community? I was determined that the school should go ahead – at almost any cost! I still had faith, based on everything Colin Hodgetts had said, and believed that we would get funding in the end, one way or another. The decision had to be made with my heart and not my head.

Another hurdle that needed to be cleared was that I could not appoint myself as teacher, as The New School project had already established itself as a democratic organisation. I would have to wait for the approval of the trustees, the parents' group, the steering group and the financial planning group. I offered my services and waited, purposely avoiding any of the meetings discussing my appointment, as I wanted it to be a democratic decision.

Finally, I was given the decision: I was to be appointed as a teacher at The New School, but they also wanted me to take the title of headteacher. I accepted the offer without hesitation (in reality there was no other way the school could open). Meanwhile my bank manager could not understand why I had in effect 'walked away' from what had become a successful nursery business built up over years, to commit what he called, in no uncertain terms, 'financial suicide'! …

CHAPTER 12

The New School Opens Against all the Odds
(September 1993)

By the first week of September, our handyman, Les, had finished white-washing the interior walls of the newly built double garage, and we'd had wall heaters and fire extinguishers professionally fitted. We'd had the fire officer, planning officer, and Social Services check they were happy with the provision before moving all of the soft play equipment out of the Rumpus Room and into the garage. Once all the large padded floor mats, wall pads, climbing frame, large barrel and other soft play equipment had been set up in their new 'room' (i.e. the garage), we were free to finish off the preparations for The New School.

What had been the nursery's Rumpus Room was going to become the main classroom base for the children of The New School. It was approximately seventeen foot long by fifteen wide. We had just a week left to get it into shape ready for the opening of the school the following Wednesday. The existing vinyl floor

120

covering would be satisfactory for the general classroom area but we needed to have some carpeting fitted where the book area would be. We already had display boards fitted around the room but they would need covering with fresh paper and a few suitable posters to make the room more appealing for the older children.

Thanks to all the fund-raising efforts and a generous donation from one of the parents, new tables, chairs and storage cabinets had been ordered weeks ago. We had been told that they would be with us in time for the new term. As the starting date was drawing close, I phoned the different suppliers. Each one gave the same reply – that they'd been struggling to meet the large capacity of school orders over the summer, and everybody wanted the new furniture to be delivered in time for the new term!

It was Monday 6th September, two days before The New School was due to open, and still no sign of the new classroom furniture. I phoned again, explaining that we were a new school and didn't have any furniture for the children. The table and chair suppliers promised we would have the delivery in time, but the cabinet supplier couldn't make any promises.

Tuesday 7th September, and by 2pm still no sign of the tables and chairs. In desperation I phoned Graham Pirt at Riverside School and explained our predicament. Thankfully he offered to lend us some tables and chairs until ours arrived. Fortunately some of the parents helped with collecting the tables and chairs, and putting them in the room. Phew!

In preparation for the big day I had promoted my deputy at the nursery to the position of nursery manager so that I could focus on running the school. In addition to myself, the trustees had appointed an assistant part-time teacher, Jane, and we also had the input of Jenny Read as a music specialist, and Sara Betteridge as the French teacher. I had been extremely creative with the timetable. We would start each day with a circle time together – a little bit like an assembly in some respects, with a special poem or theme being introduced; but it was also an opportunity for the children to discuss the plans for the day and to share thoughts and feelings. After circle time, the children would be allocated to specific groups and activities. Teaching time would be shared amongst the different groups. The part-time teacher would come in three mornings a week to concentrate essentially on the older children. One morning Jenny would come in for a few hours, see the children in smaller groups first and then meet with them all for a joint musical activity at the end. Another morning Sera Betteridge would come in, and, with the youngest children, would complete simple practical activities using a few French words, whereas she would carry out more traditional activities with the older children. She would work with the children in three different groups according to their ability. With imaginative planning, the children had a very varied curriculum with each of them being taught to their ability, and individual needs being met as much as possible. Each child would be working to an individual education plan which would be reviewed on an individual basis fortnightly.

After Dan and Nicki had gone to bed that night, I popped downstairs just to make sure everything was ready for the following morning and to put a little vase of fresh flowers on each table. Two pieces of furniture that had arrived in time were a second-hand traditional teacher's desk, now pushed up against the wall, and a second-hand blue two-drawer filing cabinet. The desk being used mainly as a storage area with confidential records such as the register kept in one of the lockable drawers, as well as an occasional place to sit when the children were not in the room. On the wall next to the desk was a notice board with a list of planned activities and groups for the week. The filing cabinet would be a place for the children to keep some of their own work and project records.

Earlier in the day, Dan and Nicki had helped me set some displays up around the room on the borrowed furniture. One display consisted of a range of practical classroom equipment such as pencils, pens, felt-tip pens, coloured pencil crayons, scissors (left- and right-handed), all neatly displayed in pots that could be easily transferred to the tables. On another tabletop was a display relating to weighing. There were balance scales, bucket scales, kitchen scales, and a range of different objects to be weighed. I had planned weight-related activities appropriate for different ages. Some of the activities would involve baking and cooking. A third display consisted of dinosaur books and plastic dinosaurs of a variety of shapes and sizes. The dinosaurs on display were being kindly lent by Dan, and I was planning to ask the other children if they'd like to bring in any more to add to the collection. I'd already organised a trip to a dinosaur exhibition in York to take place in two weeks' time. I'd bought a CD of dinosaur songs which I'd been planning to teach the children, and also intended to use at least one of the songs for movement lessons.

Dan and Nicki had also helped me set up the book corner in the area where we'd had a square of carpet fitted. With a little bit of help, Nicki had set out the books for the younger children from the enormous range of books we already had in the nursery store cupboards. Dan said he didn't need his *Thomas the Tank Engine* books any more and he'd like to give them to the school, so went upstairs to get them. By the time he'd come back down, Nicki had got tired of sorting books and was comfortably laid out on the floor cushions and had started reading instead! I had started sorting out some new books we'd bought for The New School, when Dan said he could bring down some spare Science and Space books he had, in addition to the dinosaur books he'd lent earlier.

As Dan looked across at Nicky engrossed in her book, he turned to me, saying, 'What about my *Secret Seven* books? I can always read them again in school if they're down here, and I think the other children might like them too.' I said I thought it would be a lovely idea. So Dan made three more trips upstairs to his bedroom to bring down his entire collection of Enid Blyton's *Secret Seven* books!

It was almost 10pm and I should have been thinking about getting to bed ready for the first day of The New School the next day. I found myself staring at the collection of *Secret Seven* books. We'd discovered this collection over the summer holiday period in a discount bookshop in Scarborough while staying at our caravan in Filey. On the first visit to the bookshop, Dan used his pocket money to buy two *Secret Seven*s. Back at the caravan, he read one of them from beginning to end before bedtime, and had finished the second before lunch the following day. At the time, this had appeared something of a miracle. The *Secret Seven* series really appealed to Dan, and every time we went to Scarborough he spent his pocket money on another two books. He was once again hooked on reading! Continuing to stare at these books, I was aware that, at the time, they were not considered 'politically correct', mainly due the old-fashioned sexist attitudes portrayed. I was aware that these books could be frowned upon, yet they had definitely done something for Dan that other story books hadn't achieved since he'd started school. I believe the reason for this was that the books used relatively simple vocabulary, the print was quite large, and the pages were thick within the hardback covers, giving the impression that they were 'bigger' than they actually were; and more to the point, Dan found the stories exciting. And with happy thoughts of Dan's renewed interest in reading, I went to bed.

It was 8am on 8th September 1993. The new classroom was bright and airy, and beautifully set out to give the children a warm welcome. A large bay window looked over the street, where you could see parents parking their cars and leading their very young children by hand through the secure gates into the nursery below. Another tall window overlooked the nursery playground with its combination of a concrete area, a grassed area and a large sandpit attractively outlined with upright cut-down logs. Dan and Nicki were still upstairs with Alf at that moment but would be down in a few minutes.

All of a sudden, the intercom buzzed. It was one of the nursery staff based downstairs letting me know that a delivery man had arrived with the new tables and chairs! I looked at the clock. It was ten minutes past eight and all the children would be here in a few minutes. I wasn't sure whether to be pleased about the delivery or not. If I'd had time to think, I'd have asked for the items to be stored somewhere else temporarily, but before I was aware of what was happening, the tables and chairs were being brought into the classroom. I was trying to unwrap them and get them into place as quickly as possible when The New School children started to arrive. Not exactly what I'd planned. But fortunately everybody could see the funny side! By 8.35pm the parents had left, and everything had calmed down a bit.

Although I had intended to start most days with a circle time, it seemed more appropriate today, especially after the new table fiasco, to hold it at the end of the session rather than the beginning. Therefore the children were invited to sit at the appropriate junior-sized or infant-sized table for their first activity. The older children were asked to write about their feelings regarding The New School, and the younger children were asked to draw their feelings and put a few words on their picture if they could.

When they had finished, the younger children played with the dinosaurs and looked at the dinosaur books while I sat with the older children as each of them read a dinosaur poem in turn. After discussing the poems, they started to write their own, at which point I rejoined the younger children and we talked about dinosaurs in some depth before introducing a maths sorting activity, still using the dinosaurs.

It was at this point a local press photographer arrived, followed by the presenter from Radio Humberside. It seemed like a good time to stop for our mid-morning snack.

As it was such a fine day, we all agreed to go for a walk along the riverbank after the snack. The children were encouraged to look carefully, share their existing knowledge, and ask questions.

From time to time we all stopped just to listen and then talk about what we could hear. Returning to the classroom with a collection of fallen leaves, with a view to identifying the trees, followed by leaf prints or drawings, it seemed like it had been a successful morning.

To end our very successful first day, I asked the children to pull their chairs into a circle. As soon as they were settled, I started by saying: 'We made it. We've got our new school. We've all worked really hard to get this far. I'm sure you're all going to be very happy here. We're going to start off by saying how each of us have felt about today. I've been really excited all morning. How did you feel, Emily?'

'I've been really pleased to be here. My last school was too big and noisy and I found it very hard to concentrate on my work. I think I'll like it here. I got to know some of you at the Saturday Morning Club, so that's good. I'm really looking forward to the afternoon activities, especially the horse-riding.' (Emily, age ten.)

'I'm pleased to be here too,' said Rosie (eight). 'I remember when I used to come to the nursery here when I was little, and sometimes I used to come here in the school holidays and go on some of the trips. I used to go to the same school as Emily. It was very big and very noisy and I was always getting into trouble. The other children used to call me "Specky-four-eyes" too – that really upset me.'

'Mmm, I think I might like it here,' said Andrew (five). 'Mmm, yes, that's what I think.'

'Me too,' said James (six). Asked how he felt, James smiled shyly and said, 'Good.'

'I think I'm really going to like it here,' said James's sister, Sally (seven). 'I've got my brother and my cousin, it's going to be like being in a big family.'

'Well, I used to come to the nursery here,' said Georgina (five). 'I know I'll like it here.'

'I'm really excited. I like this new room, and I liked the walk this morning,' said Nicki (four).

'I liked the walk too,' said Sean (four). 'I've been really 'cited about starting big school today!'

'I was always in trouble at my school. I hope I won't get into trouble here.' said Simon (seven). 'I used to come to nursery here too, a very long time ago – I used to really like that so I think I'll like this too.'

Whitney (nine), looking very serious, said, 'I was really unhappy at my old school, I was bullied a lot. Other children kept telling me I was fat! I hated going to school. I don't think that will happen here. At the Saturday Morning Club everybody was really kind.'

Maxine (eight) said, 'I was bullied at my old school too. I really didn't like going. I was so happy when my mum said I could come here. I used to come to the nursery here two afternoons a week when I was little.'

Last but not least, it was Dan's turn. 'I'm really pleased that Mum managed to get this new school started. At my old school some children called me "stupid" and some children called me "clever clogs" and that made me feel very unhappy. I didn't like going to my old school but I think I'll like it here …'

Epilogue

Lives were changed forever. Within weeks of the school opening some of the children became almost unrecognisable as their rounded shoulders and grim outlook on life were replaced by a confident stature, more relaxed and confident faces and happy eyes. People could hardly believe the change in the children. The learning difficulties that some of the children had experienced previously were far less of a problem in this new, nurturing environment. As well as the children changing, their parents became more confident and outgoing too – for many of them had, like me, been made to feel inadequate before this project started.

It was the commitment of all the parents, combined with the professionals involved (some who were prepared to work for low wages, and others who were more than willing to work for nothing at all), to support a project they really believed in, that kept the school going. After the first few weeks, in addition to the transformation of the children, other miracles started to happen. The first was £10,000 trust funding, with a promise of another £10,000 in twelve months' time. The second was that a sympathetic benefactor bought a disused Victorian school building, in an idyllic setting, for us to move into at the end of our first term. Looking back now, the story is hard to believe. The amount of emotional and physical energy that went into this little school was incredible. You can read the continuing story in my next book: *The Small School Years.*

At the age of seventeen, while attending Selby College, Dan received a diagnosis of 'moderate dyslexia' after an assessment with the University of Hull's Department of Psychology. The psychologist who carried out this assessment had sight of the letter I had received years previously categorically stating that Dan was definitely *not* dyslexic, and indicating that his poor self-esteem was due to our parenting skills. He was horrified!

Dan went on to take a degree in Computer Science, and has been employed ever since as a web developer. I sometimes wonder what would have happened to him if I hadn't opened the small school and had left him to struggle in mainstream education. Nicki recently obtained a First Class honours degree in International Business Studies and, at this moment in time, is juggling a job, voluntary work, and studying Spanish, while searching for her ideal career opportunity.

In my current professional role, I work very closely with parents. Over the years, I have supported numerous parents who've received letters very similar to mine. In each case, they have been left devastated by the suggestion that their child struggling in school could be due to their parenting skills being lacking in some way. Such a letter does not help the parent or the child. In many cases, the letter has been proven to be wrong, when after further investigation the child has received a diagnosis of special educational needs.

Working with a group of parents recently, one parent said,

'When there is a problem, the teachers become very defensive and seem to close ranks.' Others claimed to have felt bullied and ridiculed by teachers.

Parenting is one of the most important jobs in the world, yet one for which we receive very little training. Whereas I believe that every parent has the capacity to learn new parenting skills and strategies, they are still the expert on their own child, and I would like to see many more professionals treating parents with the respect they deserve, and listening more carefully to what they are saying. So many of the parents I work with on a day-to-day basis are at a total loss as to how to help their children. I can currently help them by teaching them strategies to help with relationships and behaviour at home but there is little I can do to address what seems to be a constant problem in most of their lives, the negative affects of attending a very large school. Behaviour problems, which are so often linked to learning difficulties, often start when children move from primary school to a much larger secondary school.

Generally schools are becoming larger and larger in an effort to save costs. Isn't it time that the true human cost of large schools be measured? Isn't it time league tables disappeared forever and schools adapted to meet the individual needs of their pupils? Isn't it time that the quality of the relationships in schools became regarded as more important than academic success? Isn't it time that parents started to be really listened to and the attitudes of some professionals towards parents be re-examined?

Having got that off my chest, I must add that there are some excellent schools that really care for all their children. There are many teachers who follow a human scale, nurturing approach towards individual children and their parents. I just wish there were more.

Some children will thrive in large schools, some will cope well with whatever life throws at them, but others will not. For some children with a problematic home-life, school can be an absolute haven, even a life-saver. But for others their personal difficulties (whether home-life or un-supported learning needs) can lead to disengagement with the school system and society. In his book *Urban Village Schools – putting relationships at the heart of the organisation and design of our secondary schools*, (2010) James Wetz writes:

Despite the very best efforts of our teachers and our education system, there is a widening gap between the young people who are achieving in our schools and the growing disaffection, alienation, and anger of a significant and increasing number of young people who leave school with few if any qualifications, little chance of worthwhile employment, little interest in further training or education beyond school, and little stake in mainstream society.

After the Conservative / Liberal Democrat coalition government was formed in 2010, plans were announced regarding the funding of new Free Schools which could be set up by parents, teachers, and voluntary groups. Comparisons were made with schools in Denmark and Charter Schools in America. In September 2011, twenty-four government-funded Free Schools were set up in the UK; the following September, another fifty-five were set up. Many more Free Schools are planning to open. It's a pity the Free Schools policy wasn't introduced when we were starting our small school, but perhaps the campaigning by Human Scale Education at that time may have contributed in some way to the politicians moving in this direction. Of course all the Free Schools will have different educational philosophies. Hopefully, though, more of them will work in partnership with parents towards nurturing each child according to their individual needs, abilities, aspirations and talents.

Regarding the new Free Schools in the UK, the government website www.education.gov.uk states:

Free Schools are all-ability state-funded schools set up in response to what local people say they want and need in order to improve education for children in their community.

The right school can transform a child's life and help them achieve things they may never have imagined. Through the Free Schools programme it is now much easier for talented and committed teachers, charities, parents and education experts to open schools to address real demand within an area.

Dr Tony Breslin, Chair of Human Scale Education (2010-2014) says 'Of course, the Free Schools programme is controversial – not all are likely to be set up by groups of individuals that are of progressive intent and, in some cases, a new Free School may damage existing schools, including those working positively in the most challenging of circumstances, but elsewhere, the initiative is leading to the establishment of schools that are modelling human scale practice and the opening of schools in areas that are currently not served by extensive existing provision.

Against this background, and while grappling with the merits of, and challenges posed by, the Free School programme, HSE is currently working with a small number of Free Schools that are committed to the principles and values of Human Scale Education. Hopefully, more Free Schools will embrace human scale perspectives and add to the footprint of human scale practice that HSE is developing across a range of educational settings.'

As this book goes to press, Human Scale Education is in the process of re-structuring. Robin Precey (Director of Leadership and Management at Canterbury Christchurch University) was appointed as the new Chair in April, 2014 along with a new board consisting of twelve trustees. Plans are being made for an event to be held in 2015 to celebrate both Human Scale Education's thirtieth year and its official re-launch. To find out more please visit HSE's website: www.hse.org.uk; or the HSE links on my blog www.diarynotesonlife.blogspot.co.uk.

If you would like to receive updates regarding my next book, *The Small School Years*, and subsequent book, *An Educational Journey*, visit my aforementioned blog or website www.rosalynspencer.co.uk. In the meantime, I have listed some organisations overleaf that may be of use to parents, teachers and childcare professionals who are looking for answers when children are struggling …

Useful Contacts

(United Kingdom)

Anti-bullying Alliance
National Children's Bureau
8 Wakley Street
London
EC1V 7QE
www.anti-bullyingalliance.org.uk

ADHD
www.adhd.org.uk

The Asperger's Syndrome Foundation
c/o Littlestone Golding
Eden House
Reynolds Road
Beaconsfield
HP9 2FL
www.aspergerfoundation.org.uk

British Dyslexia Association
Unit 8 Bracknell Beeches
Old Bracknell Lane
Bracknell
RG12 7BW
Tel: 0845 251 9003
www.bdadyslexia.org.uk

Dyslexia Action
Park House
Wick Road
Egham
Surrey
TW20 0HH
Tel: 01784 222 300
www.dyslexiaaction.org.uk

Dyspraxia Foundation
8 West Alley
Hitchin
Herts
SG5 1EG
Tel: 01462 455016
www.dyspraxiafoundation.org.uk

Education Otherwise
PO Box 3761
Swindon
SN2 9GT
www.educationotherwise.net

Human Scale Education
Unit 8 Fairseat farm
Stoke Hill
Chew Stoke
Bristol
BS40 8XF
Tel: 01275 332516
www.hse.org.uk

The National Autistic Society
393 City Road
London
EC1V 1NG
Tel: 020 7833 2299
Helpline: 0808 800 4104
www.autism.org.uk

National Parent Partnership Network
8 Wakley Street
London
EC1V 7QE
www.parentpartnership.org.uk

Nurture Group Network
CAN Mezzanine
49 – 51 East Road
Old Street
London
N1 6AH
www.nurturegroups.org

Steiner Waldorf Schools Fellowship Ltd
11 Church Street
Stourbridge
DY8 1LT
Tel: 01384 374116
www.steinerwaldorf.org.uk

About the Author

Rosalyn Spencer has an MA in Education by Research. With over 25 years teaching experience, her lifetime's work has involved finding ways of helping individuals to succeed – ranging from young children struggling to survive in mainstream education, and teenagers in care, to setting up and running a children's nursery and then a non-fee paying 'alternative' small school.

Rosalyn has had numerous articles about education and parenting published in magazines including *Natural Parent, Nursery World* and *The Green Parent*. In 1999 she was commissioned by Human Scale Education to write a report entitled *15 Small Schools.*

Both her children have now left home, and Rosalyn remarried in 2011. She spends her free time taking photographs, playing classical guitar, swimming, and of course, writing. For more information visit:

www.rosalynspencer.co.uk;

www.diarynotesonlife.blogspot.co.uk;

or email: contact@rosalynspencer.co.uk

Acknowledgements

I would like to thank the following individuals who helped me on my journey towards publishing this, my first book, in a series of three: *Why I Started a Small School...*

Both my children: when they were young, for being the main reason for the small school; and more recently, Dan for setting up my website (while he was still a Computer Science student at University); and Nicki for painstakingly reading my manuscript drafts, and taking time to comment on every aspect.

My husband, Ian Johnson, whose help and encouragement led to me finally achieving my goal.

My parents, Alf and Vera Mayne, for agreeing to be guarantors for the business loan that enabled us to set up the nursery. Alf's parents, Alf (Senior) and Ivy Spencer, who gave endless hours of support, especially in the early days of setting up the nursery.

Colin Hodgetts, Fiona Carnie and Satish Kumar of Human Scale Education for providing me with the vision and support to set up a small school.

Kevin Holloway, for being a key player in supporting the small school from its initial conception, throughout its lifetime, and beyond, including valuable contributions to this book.

Rick Hayward, for the time he spent reading an earlier draft and offering invaluable advice.

ACKNOWLEDGEMENTS

Sharon Whitehead for encouraging my writing.

James Wetz and Tony Breslin, the former Director and former Chair (respectfully) of Human Scale Education, for their contributions to the Epilogue; and additionally, to James Wetz for writing the Foreword.

Martin Ouvry of Writers' Workshop for completing a professional critique of an earlier manuscript, offering useful advice, and copy-editing the final version.

All the staff at Matador, for their help and support towards the publication of this book.

Satish Kumar, Stuart McBurney, Steve Gosse, Ann Hickey, Martin Ouvry, Colin Hodgetts, Kevin Holloway, Dr Tony Breslin and Geoff Needham for kindly offering endorsements.

To my other pre-publication readers including Jean Kitchen, Sam Crawford, Steve Ulyat, Dennis Rock, Mary O'Connell, Chris Robinson, and Kate Harrison for all your encouraging comments, and useful suggestions.

My sincere thanks and gratitude to everyone mentioned here, and apologies to anyone I may have accidentally forgotten to mention.